25 Bicycle Tours in Pennsylvania's Lancaster and Chester Counties

25 Bicycle Tours in Pennsylvania's Lancaster and Chester Counties

FRED A. COX

Scenic Rides
in Pennsylvania's
Amish and Horse
Country

The Countryman Press
Woodstock, Vermont

25 Bicycle Tours in Pennsylvania's Lancaster and Chester Counties

ISBN 978-0-88150-884-0

Interior photographs by the author
Cover and interior design by Bodenweber Design
Composition by Chelsea Cloeter
Maps by Paul Woodward, © The Countryman Press

Published by The Countryman Press, P.O. Box 748, Woodstock, VT 05091

Distributed by WW. Norton & Company, Inc., 500 Fifth Avenue, New York, NY 10110

Printed in the United States of America

10 9 8 7 6 5 4 3 2 1

This book is dedicated to my mother
and to the memory of my father,
Jeanne W. and Fred W. Cox,
who bought me my first bikes and allowed me
the freedom to ride them.

25 Bike Tours in Pennsylvania's Lancaster & Chester Counties

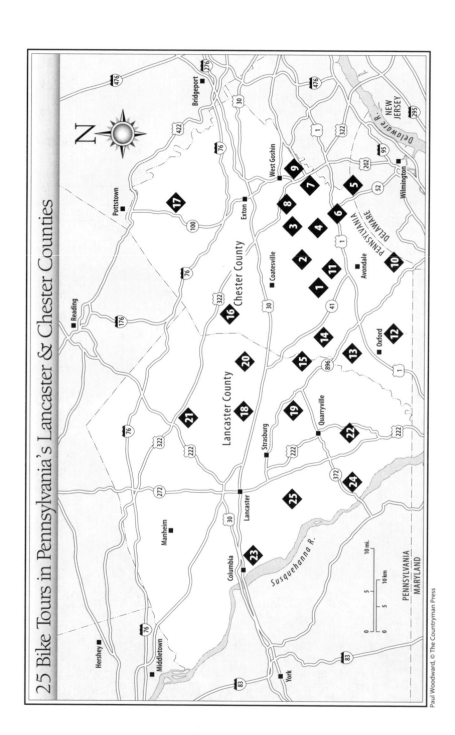

Paul Woodward, © The Countryman Press

CONTENTS

Chester County

WEST MARLBOROUGH TOWNSHIP – HORSE COUNTRY

BRANDYWINE VALLEY

WEST CHESTER

SOUTHERN CHESTER COUNTY

WESTERN CHESTER COUNTY

NORTHERN CHESTER COUNTY

Lancaster County

AMISH COUNTRY

SUSQUEHANNA VALLEY

PREFACE My first adventure on a bicycle happened when I was about five years old. I can still feel the thrill of it, like my first rappel or the first Telemark turns of a new ski season. I had inherited a bike from one of my cousins, and despite my father's earnest attempts at teaching me to ride it, I just couldn't keep it upright. A day came when two of my slightly older friends were going to ride over to "the armory," which had a large, paved parking lot, and they invited me along. The trouble was that I couldn't ride. I *really* wanted to go, so I pushed my little bike up the alleyway behind our yard until I reached the top of the steep hill. After running with the bike for a few steps, I jumped on and held the handlebars, keeping the front wheel straight. It worked just the way it was supposed to, and after coasting down the hill I stepped on the foot brake, joined my friends, and entered a new world. I think that one reason this memory stands out so much for me is that I was kind of a timid kid at that age and not much given to acts of daring.

As a child, a bike meant freedom and adventure, but when I was a teen, nobody rode bikes, so I ended up getting my first ten-speed when I was in medical school. My wife and I spent a month after our wedding riding about a thousand miles in Germany on two Peugeot U08s, and since then we've ridden many thousands of miles in the United States and Canada. Our children grew up riding bikes, and we took them on as many rides as their time and capabilities allowed.

When we lived in the New England countryside, my sons used to tease me, saying that I would drive a hundred miles to ride a bike on a road just like the one in front of our house. It took a few years, I think, before they really understood, but ultimately they did. Our family rode a lot together and spent many pleasant hours on back roads and woodland trails. At one time I recall that we had 10 bikes in our garage; hanging nearby were 14 pairs of skis. One of my proudest moments happened after my two sons and I had ridden down a steep singletrack on our mountain bikes. My older son stopped and said, "Old man, you crazy!" It just doesn't get any better than that for a middle-aged man.

Riding the back roads, smelling the smells, hearing the sounds, feeling the wind and weather, meeting the people, and enjoying vitality with our labored breathing and pounding hearts, my wife, Margaret, and I would sometimes pause and say, "Can you believe this is good for us, too?" It seems that something so much fun should have a price, but it doesn't, does it.

I hope everyone who takes these rides enjoys them as much as I did, especially while standing up on the pedals, stretching out over the handlebars on a 72-degree dry summer day, and cruising down a hill on a two-wheeled magic carpet.

ACKNOWLEDGMENTS First I would like to thank my wife, Margaret, my sons, Hans and Jeff, and my daughter, Elizabeth, for giving me the time and freedom to ride and for making many of these rides so much more fun with their very presence.

I am also grateful for the generosity and friendship of Clinton Hubbard, Leslee and Lou Kaplan, Jan and Craig Bakken, and Ann and Jack Rule, who have helped me to write this book. Special thanks go to Reid Bakken for his graphics expertise.

It wouldn't do not to mention my riding buddies Rick Craven, Roy Proujansky, John Yindra, Chuck Maxin, and Richard Brousell, who shared many of these rides with me while I was first exploring this countryside.

To my old friend and publishing coach, Lucy Hedrick, I owe all of the practical knowledge I needed to bring this book from the germ of an idea to print and paper.

I especially appreciate all the work and assistance of Kermit Hummel, Lisa Sacks, and Justine Rathbun, my editors at The Countryman Press, without whom this book would never have made it into print.

RIDES AT A GLANCE

RIDE	REGION	TERRAIN
1. Runnymede Road—Saint Malachi Church	West Marlborough Township	Rolling hills
2. Stargazer's Stone	West Marlborough Township	Rolling hills
3. Apple Grove Road—King Ranch Land	West Marlborough Township	Rolling hills with a couple of strenuous climbs
4. Longwood North	Brandywine Valley	Rolling hills
5. Longwood South into Delaware	Brandywine Valley	Mostly flat; some rolling hills
6. Hillendale Road	Brandywine Valley	Rolling hills
7. Brandywine Battlefield	Brandywine Valley	One long, gradual uphill near beginning; flat along the river; rolling hills elsewhere
8. Ground Hog College Road	West Chester	Rolling hills; short section of rough pavement
9. Westtown School	West Chester	Rolling hills in the countryside; urban in the city of West Chester
10. Arc Corner	Southern Chester County	Rolling hills; some heavily wooded sections
11. West Grove	Southern Chester County	Rolling hills
12. Nottingham	Southern Chester County	Rolling hills
13. Oxford—Lincoln University	Southern Chester County	Rolling hills

DISTANCE	DIFFICULTY	HIGHLIGHTS
13.5 miles	Easy	Saint Malachi Church, large horse farms, large natural spring
20.7 miles	Easy	Stargazer's Stone, Embreeville Mill, covered bridge, Brandywine Creek, horse farms
36.6 miles	Moderate	Dramatic and expansive views of old King Ranch Land, covered bridge
16.9 miles	Easy	Longwood Gardens, open countryside
22.5 or 27.4 miles	Easy	Longwood Gardens, Brandywine River, Delaware "chateau country," Delaware Museum of Natural History, Winterthur, Hagley Museum
21.1 miles	Easy	Very nice, long country road; Brandywine Polo Club fields, New Garden Flying Field (stunt flyers)
17.3 miles	Easy to moderate	Revolutionary War battlefield, Brandywine River Museum, Birmingham Meetinghouse and cemetery, scenery of the Upper Brandywine Valley
17.4 miles	Easy	Upper Brandywine Valley
15.7 miles	Moderate	West Chester University, Westtown School
22.5 miles	Moderate	White Clay Creek Preserve, Arc Corner, Indian town, meetinghouse
19.8 miles	Easy	Woodlands and open countryside
22.8 miles	Easy	Ride in two states, covered bridge, some Amish farms
19 miles	Easy	Open farmland, historic African American university

RIDE	REGION	TERRAIN
14. Cochranville	Western Chester County	Rolling hills
15. Atglen—Bailey Bridge	Western Chester County	Rolling hills; mostly flat
16. Hibernia Park	Western Chester County	Rolling hills
17. Nantmeal Village—Horseshoe Trail	Northern Chester County	Rolling hills
18. Strasburg North	Amish Country	Mostly flat
19. Strasburg South	Amish Country	Rolling hills
20. White Horse Road	Amish Country	Gentle, rolling hills
21. Katze Boucle Weeg	Amish Country	Rolling hills; one short, sharp hill
22. Robert Fulton House	Amish Country	Rolling hills
23. Sam Lewis State Park	Susquehanna Valley	Level along the river, with a strenuous climb to the park
24. Muddy Run—Holtwood Dam	Susquehanna Valley	Hilly
25. Safe Harbor	Susquehanna Valley	Rolling hills

DISTANCE	DIFFICULTY	HIGHLIGHTS
17 miles	Easy	Horse farms, open countryside
21.3 miles	Easy	Old town of Atglen, East Branch of Octoraro Creek, covered bridge
23.9 miles	Easy	Historic park, Lancaster County, migratory birds at nearby Marsh Creek State Park
26.8 miles	Easy	Old village of Nantmeal, nearby St. Peters Village, open countryside
17 miles	Easy	Strasburg attractions, Amish farms
25 miles	Easy to moderate	Strasburg attractions, Amish farmland, expansive views of countryside
17.8 miles	Easy	Amish farming country, Amish school-houses, horse-drawn carriages
19.2 miles	Easy to moderate	Amish farms, covered bridge
21.4 miles	Easy	Fulton birthplace, Amish farms, ride along West Branch of Octoraro Creek
23.2 miles	Moderate	Spectacular views of the southern Susquehanna River from the summit of Mount Pisgah in the state park
13.1 miles	Moderate	Holtwood hydroelectric dam, Muddy Run Recreation Park, view of river from observation area, frequent sightings of bald eagles
30.8 miles	Easy to moderate	Descents and climbs in the Susque-hanna River Valley, town of Safe Harbor, Neff's Mill Covered Bridge, Strasburg attractions

INTRODUCTION A fortunate combination of geographic and historical circumstances creates a nearly ideal region for bicycling in Lancaster and Chester counties in southeastern Pennsylvania. The land is part of a thousand-mile-long belt stretching from the Palisades along the Hudson River in New York to central Alabama. This is the Piedmont, a vast plain of undulating hills dissected by streams and a few rivers, bounded by the inland limit of the coastal plain to the east and the foothills of the Appalachian Mountain chain to the west.

The early settlers founded ports at the mouths of the rivers that reach the Atlantic coast, then boated up the rivers until they encountered impassable rapids or waterfalls. They founded settlements at this "fall line"—which forms the eastern boundary of the Piedmont—to trade with the interior. As settlement expanded toward the Susquehanna River, numerous small communities sprang up to serve the growing population of farmers and loggers. These communities were connected by wagon roads that have evolved into the many small country roads now available for bicycling.

The climate in this part of the Piedmont is moderate, allowing for year-round riding, with at least 180 frost-free days per year and sunshine on an average of 260 days per year. There is no dry or wet season on the Piedmont; an average of 40–50 inches of rain per year falls on this area and is well distributed throughout the seasons. This climate and the fertile soil eroded from ancient mountaintops create ideal conditions for farming and grazing, accounting for much of the area's picturesque scenery.

This is a region of roughly 1,700 square miles, larger than Rhode Island. Its terrain of rolling hills and streams, forested land, and manicured farms is within easy driving distance of the surrounding metro-

Horse farm in Chester County

politan areas. There is much of historical interest as well: Revolutionary War battlefields, Quaker meetinghouses, ancient farmsteads, and
museums. The roads, some of which were laid out more than two hundred years ago, allow bicyclists to avoid the main highways and to
experience the peace and quiet of this lush countryside.

The majority of the rides are concentrated in southern and central
Chester County and southeastern Lancaster County, where I think the
best and safest rides are. Many of these rides can be connected into
longer rides, and they can be improvised upon using local maps. The
countryside is sufficiently varied that these rides can be done over and
over again without monotony. Sometimes just riding one of the routes
in the opposite direction makes the experience entirely different.

With that said, there are a few issues you should be aware of
regarding bike riding in the area, bike safety and equipment, and this
book's rides.

About the Area

SOME PROBLEMS WITH BACKCOUNTRY BICYCLING Following routes on back roads presents some challenges, including:

- Road names often change when crossing county lines.
- The same road may have two or three different names along its course.
- Signage may not indicate changes in road names.
- Road names on maps may be different from signage.
- Signage may be missing.
- At an intersection, the road on the left may have a different name from the road on the right; only one of them may be included on the sign.
- Numbered roads often also have names, and signage is inconsistent.

I have chosen to use the names featured on the road signs rather than those on the maps, because that is what will confront you while you are riding these routes. To alleviate confusion, I have at times pointed out these inconsistencies where I feel they may mislead you. In cases of absent signage, I have used Google Maps as the final arbiter.

It is advantageous to schedule rides around traffic patterns. Some rides, particularly those in tourist-friendly Amish country, are best done on weekdays or on weekend mornings before the traffic picks up. Others are best done on weekend mornings or weekdays 10–3 to avoid commuting rush hours. The West Chester rides and the ride into Delaware (ride 5) on PA 52 and DE 100 are examples of these.

THE AMISH There are Amish and Mennonites in various parts of North America, including Canada, but there is a singular concentration of them in Lancaster and Chester counties. You will see them mostly in eastern and southern Lancaster County and western and southern Chester County. On their large, neat farms, they perform their work using mules and large draft horses. They do not use electricity and do not have televisions or telephones. For the most part, they do not drive automobiles, but some Mennonites will drive cars that are stripped of adornment and painted black.

The Amish don't have churches but rather take turns holding services in their homes and barns. On Sunday you may see them traveling to services in their buggies, their wheel rims polishing the pavement. At times you will see Amish children riding bicycles, scooters, or roller skates on the roads. The children will often ride ponies bareback, but the adults drive wagons and carriages.

Old Order Amish are descendents of Swiss-German Anabaptists who immigrated to Pennsylvania in the early 18th century to escape religious persecution. Known for their plain, frugal, and hardworking lifestyle, they do not like to be photographed, so it would be impolite to point a camera at them. Taking photos from a distance is more discreet.

I think their presence tends to make the back roads safer for bicyclists, because area motorists are accustomed to dealing with pedestrian and horse-drawn vehicles.

About Equipment

As most of these rides are in rural areas without services, you will need, at the least, two water bottle cages and two 16-ounce plastic water bottles. A rear carrier with elastic cords is handy for carrying extra clothing, and you should have a pump and small tool kit that fits in a pouch beneath the seat. The tool kit should contain a tire-patch kit, tire irons, a multi-tool or Swiss Army knife, and a small set of Allen wrenches to fit the screws on your machine. I also carry a chain rivet tool and a spoke wrench. For longer trips, a couple of spare spokes that fit your wheel can be taped to your pump. A small roll of electrical or duct tape can also be handy. If you are traveling in a group, these items can be distributed among several riders.

A can of pepper spray can be mounted on your handlebars; you won't have time to dig it out of your pack when you really need it. Additionally, a front-mounted carry bag with a clear plastic map window is very handy and keeps your map dry if it rains.

A rearview mirror should be mounted on your handlebars or helmet. Your ears will pick up the first car passing in a procession; your mirror will pick up the others that are in the sound shadow of the first. A mirror is also handy to see if your riding companions are still with you.

Most riders find that a cycle computer is useful. These are available with multiple and elaborate functions, but all you really need is an odometer and a speedometer.

Lastly, it's a good idea to keep a small first-aid kit in your car. Tailor your kit to the common bike injuries, mainly scrapes and scratches. A clean washcloth, a bar of soap, a tube of antibiotic ointment, some sterile gauze, Band-Aids, and adhesive tape should do.

About Safety

Bike riding on roads is inherently dangerous, but you can reduce risk. Risk, alas, cannot be eliminated, but only reduced. The unexpected happens despite caution, and many bicyclists have "road rash" and healed fractures to attest to this. To stay safer on the road, consider the following:

- Always wear a helmet. If you are at all skeptical, try this: hold a cantaloupe at the level your head would be if you were on a bike and let it drop to the pavement. That's what would happen to your brain if you were not wearing a helmet during a fall.

- Wear bright-colored clothing or a small reflective vest. The most visible color available now is a Day-Glo green.

- Equip your bike with reflectors, front, rear, and side. Sometimes it is a small thing that attracts a motorist's attention and saves your life. Riders of recumbent bicycles would be well advised to also display a bright, highly visible flag attached to their machine by a 6-foot-long fiberglass pole. Recumbents are lower to the ground and not easily seen by drivers who are not accustomed to looking for them. The recumbent rider's bright clothing is also not visible from the rear, being hidden by the seat back.

- Attach a flashing light to the rear of your seat post or bike rack. You can turn it on when passing through tunnels or covered bridges or in conditions of dim light or rain. These lights are visible at surprisingly great distances.

- Always ride on the right side of the road with traffic—never against traffic. Don't, however, ride so close to the right side that you risk slipping off the road surface and crashing.

- Don't wear headphones or listen to your iPod. Your safety depends almost as much on your hearing as it does on your vision. Without your hearing, you can't be aware of the snarling dog trying to run you down, the school bus coming up behind you, or the second or third car in the line passing you.

- Be aware of road surfaces. Country roads make for pleasant riding, but their surfaces vary. Shoulders get washed out, potholes and large cracks appear in asphalt, and washboarding occurs on gravel and dirt roads. Gravel and sand tend to accumulate on curves and at the bottoms of hills, so when you see them, slow down and avoid turning on them. The grooves of railroad tracks and the lattices of storm drains are just the right size to capture a bike tire and send you sprawling. Wait for traffic to clear, and then ride around drains; approach railroad tracks to cross them perpendicularly. If they look too rough, it is best to dismount and walk across them to avoid a spill or damage to your machine. Bridge decks can also be a hazard:

sometimes they are made of steel mesh and can be slippery, and covered-bridge decks are often composed of long wooden planks running in the direction of travel, leaving wide gaps due to shrinkage across the grain over the years. Again, it is safer to dismount and walk these sections. Longer covered bridges can be quite dark, and since you will probably be wearing sunglasses, you won't see as well in the dim light. Put on your rear flasher and walk them, especially if you can't clearly see the road surface.

- There are a few old bridges across some streams and the upper Brandywine River that present the only situation in which I think obstructing traffic is the safest course. The bridges in question are short and narrow, with chest-high abutments on both sides. There are no shoulders, and there is just enough room for two cars to pass in opposite directions. If there is any traffic, it isn't even safe to walk across. While riding or walking on the right margin, you could easily be crushed against the side. Wait for traffic to thin out, and then ride right down the center of your lane until you've completed the crossing. That's the safest thing to do in that situation.

- Another special local hazard is the locust trees in Chester County, which produce beautiful blossoms in the springtime but have rugged thorns, some of which are 2 inches long. Avoid running over downed branches in the road. Also avoid turning on wet leaves in the fall, which can be as slippery as ice.

- Use standard hand signals when you are riding in a group or whenever there are any vehicles around. The left arm pointed out straight signals a left turn; the left arm crooked upward at the elbow, forearm pointed upward, signals a right turn; and the left arm crooked downward at the elbow, forearm pointed down, signals a stop.

- For your own safety, make it a habit to make all left turns after coming to a complete stop, especially in hilly country. You may not hear or see a speeding car approaching from either direction, or a driver behind you may behave erratically and choose that moment to pass you.

- Practice "defensive bicycling": expect every driver to do the stupidest, most dangerous, and most discourteous thing imaginable. By far, drivers pose the greatest danger to bicyclists. I have thought of making a bumper sticker: THE MORE DRIVERS I MEET, THE MORE I LIKE BIKE PATHS. I have ridden about 50,000 miles in Europe and North America, and all of the instances in which I felt that my life was threatened have occurred because of the behavior of drivers. Fortunately, most drivers are courteous and will give you enough berth, but there are some who will do outrageously dangerous things. Stay alert.

- Keep a wary eye on dogs. Dogs are somewhat like drivers, only less dangerous. In the country you will encounter unleashed dogs, and some of them will chase you. There is something about a bike that seems to drive some dogs absolutely mad. Fortunately, most are just going through the motions of defending their territory. They will bark and snarl at you and run along next to you, but most will not actually attack you. Your greatest danger from these dogs would be allowing yourself to be startled or panicked and falling off your bike. Riding downhill or on the level, you can easily outrun dogs, but even on a gentle upgrade they can catch you. If you feel immediately threatened, stop, dismount, and place your machine between you and the dog. Talk authoritatively and in a friendly voice; most will back off. If an aggressive dog fails to back off, try walking slowly down the road out of the dog's territory, keeping your bike between you and the animal. If you persistently encounter such an animal, it is best to change your route.

About the Rides

This book includes 25 of my favorite rides in this region; there are many more. As you study county maps and atlases (I have recommended some at the end of the Introduction), you may invent more of your own. Some may be longer variants of these 25, which I have deliberately kept short so as not to discourage or intimidate older riders or bicyclists with children. Not all of these rides are suitable for children, however, but some do include shorter segments that are wonderful for children old enough to maintain a steady course on the road. For example, the segment of Runnymede, Thouron Road, and Big Spring Road in ride 1 is wonderful for younger riders, and the segment of ride 8 including Broad Run Road is also good. You can choose shorter segments of many of these rides for your younger kids without having to do the whole ride.

Two bicyclists make a new friend in the country.

All of these rides can be done on a road bike. There are a few short sections of rough pavement, however, but these can be ridden safely by reducing speed. All of the rough sections that existed at the time these rides were mapped have been noted in the ride descriptions.

PARKING   Finding a safe place to park can be challenging, and some creativity is often required. In general, you should keep the following in mind. Never park on the shoulder of a heavily traveled road. Even on a lightly traveled road, always make certain that you car is well off the road. Sometimes you will be able to find a parking area or pullout along the side of the road. If need be, put your flashers on and get out of the car to make certain the right-hand side of the space is stable so you won't get stuck or have a flat tire. I'll allow you to imagine how it is that I know this.

Public parks are fair game, as are schools when classes are not in session (unless otherwise posted). Always observe and respect NO PARK-ING signs. In smaller communities it is also possible to park on the street unless signs indicate otherwise. Bicyclists should always respect the rights of property owners and be mindful of how inconvenient it would be to return from a nice bike ride to find that their car had been towed. On all days except Sunday, church parking lots are usually suitable, as are the lots of post offices and municipal buildings outside of regular office hours.

Commercial lots are more problematic, but sometimes parking on the farthest perimeter of a business lot is acceptable. In the country, there are often small shops with relatively large lots. You can sometimes go into the shop, buy a sports drink or a snack, and strike up a conversation with the owner. If you ask, you will almost certainly be allowed to park there for a few hours.

Never park in front of a farm gate. The gate may be clear when you get there, but someone at that very moment may be driving a piece of farm machinery several slow miles and be planning to enter the field through that gate. Imagine the farmer's annoyance.

Oh, and be sure to make a careful note of where you parked. Write it down if necessary. I have included the GPS coordinates of the starting points for all of the rides in this book.

TIME ESTIMATES   I have not included time estimates in the ride descriptions because riders' capabilities are so varied. A fit rider can easily do a 16- or 17-mile ride in an hour or less. Most recreational bicyclists average between 10 and 12 miles per hour in rolling hills. There is also the time spent on stops to take photos, eat snacks, or just enjoy the view. I think that most riders will want to allow about two hours for a 20-mile ride.

DISTANCES   I have measured these routes using cycle computers and car odometers, and the measurements are only as accurate as those technologies allow. Watch the signs and carry a photocopy of the route map with you. I last measured all of these rides in October 2008 and remeasured some sections in May 2009. Thereafter, I verified road names on Google Maps. In the country, however, roads may sometimes be closed and bridges may sometimes be washed out. Road closures have been a particular problem over the past 20 years in the Upper Brandywine River Valley, where the closures have protected nature preserves. Some rural roads will appear on local maps but may no longer be available for travel. Sometimes a bridge will be closed to vehicles while it is under repair, but you may still be able to walk across it with a bicycle. If you run into something like this on one of your rides, you will, of course, have to recalculate your distances.

COMBINING RIDES While vigorous bicyclists may consider these rides to be short, I have deliberately made it easy to combine many of these rides into much longer excursions. It is simple to combine any of the rides that share a common starting point; for example, rides 1, 2, and 3; rides 4 and 5; rides 8 and 9; and rides 18, 19, and 25. A little study of local maps will reveal easy connections among many of the other rides; for example, rides 4, 5, 6, 7, 8, and 9. I think only rides 17, 23, and 24 cannot be connected with other rides in this book.

Useful Maps and Atlases

- *Chester County, PA: Street and Road Map.* Doylestown, PA: Alfred B. Patton, Inc., 1992.

- *Franklin's Street and Zip Code Atlas of the Western Suburbs Including The Main Line: Chester County . . . Delaware County.* 2nd ed. King of Prussia, PA: Franklin Maps, 1986.

- *Lancaster County, PA: Pennsylvania Dutch Country Street and Road Map.* Doylestown, PA: Alfred B. Patton, Inc., 1993.

- *Pennsylvania Atlas and Gazetteer.* 10th ed. Yarmouth, ME: DeLorme Mapping Company, 2007.

Chester County

Large horse pastures are common in Chester County.

WHEN YOU FIRST DRIVE into the south-central part of Chester County, you will probably wonder, as I did, how all this open land exists so close to major population centers. When you are accustomed to the bustle and crowding of suburbia and strip malls, your first sight of miles-long views of open land can be surprising. For some perspective, the population density of Philadelphia County is more than 11,000 people per square mile, while that of West Marlborough Township is a little more than 50. This did not happen by accident. There is a reason this landscape doesn't look like that along US 1 or US 30.

Chester County is very different from Lancaster County. If the defining image of the latter is the Amish man in his buggy driving past his neat farm, that of the former is a group of thoroughbred horses grazing in an immense pasture behind a white board fence. At the edge of the pasture is a stream marked by the brilliant white upper trunks of giant sycamore trees. Chester County also presents a diverse landscape contrasting the deeply wooded Upper Brandywine River Valley with the huge, open grazing pastures of the county's many horse farms, which eventually give way to Amish farms as you travel westward. It is more colorful in the springtime, proffering a gorgeous palette of flowering trees in contrast to the brown monotony of the fallow spring croplands of Lancaster County farms.

Chester was one of the three original Pennsylvania counties created by William Penn in 1682. Over the next century it lost much territory as pieces of it were carved out for new counties like Lancaster. Today it has an area of 760 square miles, much of which remains rural.

In the east, suburban developments have taken over much of the land, and in the north there is much commercial activity. The rides in this section purposely avoid those parts of the county in favor of the southern and western countryside. Only ride 9 crosses US 202 to the east to tour the woodlands and open country east of West Chester, while ride 17 takes you to a unique section of the north. I think some of the finest bicycle riding in the entire country is to be found on Chester County's back roads.

Two of the rides, 8 and 9, take you for short stretches through West Chester, the county seat. Ride 5 takes you south into Delaware and turns around just north of the city of Wilmington. Otherwise, all of these rides are rural in character, taking you through some of the nicest countryside you will see anywhere.

The aboriginal inhabitants of this area were the Lenni-Lenape, an Algonquian people who lived in the current state of New Jersey and along the Delaware River Valley. This is the tribe that negotiated the Walking Treaty with William Penn. Ride 10 allows you to visit the site of one of their ancient villages.

Considering its proximity to the greater Philadelphia area, the large tracts of open land in Chester County are striking. The Brandywine Conservancy alone has permanently protected more than 40,000 acres. Other philanthropic groups and private individuals have preserved the remainder, as has the county itself with its parks. If the rural landscape of Lancaster County looks the way it does because of the religious faith of its inhabitants, the Chester County countryside looks the way it does because of wealthy people acting either as individuals or through foundations and conservancies. Chester County has the highest per capita and median income of any of Pennsylvania's counties, and it shows on the landscape.

The number of horse farms in the county is actually increasing, a fact you will find comforting as you take these rides. I remember showing some of these farms to my daughter, who, like most girls of her age, loved horses, and telling her that this is how rich people *spend* their money, not how they *make* it. The resources it takes to keep this beautiful land open are staggering, but you and I don't have to own any of it to enjoy it. We can secure our bikes on our cars and take these rides.

You can stop next to these pastures, and sometimes horses, generally curious animals, will come over to the fence and see what you're all about. Please don't be tempted to feed them anything. They are very valuable and on special feed, and anything you give them might make them sick. Also, if you're not used to being around horses, you might not realize that some of them bite—and I don't mean nibble. Don't make the mistake of extending your fingers in the direction of a horse's mouth. All of these farms are private property, so please respect the rights of the property owners and do not trespass.

WEST MARLBOROUGH TOWNSHIP— HORSE COUNTRY

Stream crossing Runnymede Road

IF YOU WANT A TASTE of the heart of horse country in Pennsylvania, try the three rides in this section. They share a starting point in the parking lot of Chapel Road Baptist Church in Doe Run. Suitable parking areas are hard to find in this rural area, and this one gets the job done.

A lot of the pasturage seen on these rides is part of what once was King Ranch, an immense cattle operation based in Texas that at one time owned 15 million acres worldwide. In 1946 the ranch began to purchase fattening range in Chester County, which soon grew to 17,000 acres, or about 3.5 percent of the total land area of the county. Texas cattle were brought to these pastures because of the quality of the grass and proximity to large East Coast markets. In the 1980s this land was broken up, and much of it was purchased by the Brandywine Conservancy. Some was protected entirely from development, and some was sold as large estates with conservation easements. Much of the countryside that bicyclists will see on this and some of the other nearby rides was once part of this tract.

How did all of this land happen to be available for purchase by the King Ranch in 1946? Lammot du Pont, president of the DuPont company in the 1920s and '30s, was concerned about the purity of Wilmington, Delaware's, drinking water. To protect the Brandywine River watershed he purchased more than 8,000 acres in the upper valley forming Buck and Doe Run Farm. It was this land that formed a large part of the King Ranch land purchase in 1946.

Much of the time, these rides meander along the shady roads by tributaries of the West Branch of the Brandywine River, providing nice contrast to the open country. Along these streams stand the ruins of old mills, recalling a distant past when water power was used in local industry. You will cross two covered bridges on these rides: the Speakman Bridge number one on ride 2 and the Harmony Hill (Gibson) Bridge on ride 3. There are also two others in this area known as the "twin bridges": Speakman Bridge number two (the Mary Ann Pyle Bridge) and the Hayes Clark Bridge. These are on private land and may be visited only with the permission of the Brandywine Conservancy.

Because of the rural and isolated nature of these roads, there are almost no services of any kind. It is best to make sure your machine is in good shape and that you are adequately provisioned with food and water before you get off the main roads.

Interesting Reading

www.chester.pa-roots.com/townships/west_marlborough_twp.htm (historical essay)

Bicycle Shops

The Downingtown Bicycle Shop, 833 West Lancaster Avenue, Downingtown; 610-269-5626

For more bicycle shops, see the West Chester section.

1

Runnymede Road—
Saint Malachi Church

- **DISTANCE:** 13.5 miles

- **TERRAIN/DIFFICULTY:** Rolling hills, open countryside, short stretch of rough pavement; easy

- **START:** Parking lot of Chapel Road Baptist Church on Chapel Road in Doe Run

- **GPS COORDINATES OF START:** N39 54.863' / W75 49.332'

- **GETTING THERE/PARKING:** Take PA 82 to Doe Run and turn on PA 841, which intersects PA 82 from the south and ends there. Take the first right turn on Chapel Road and look for the church on the left side at 0.1 mile. Please do not park here during Sunday services.

- **HIGHLIGHTS:** Saint Malachi Church, large horse estates, a natural spring

This is listed as the number one ride in this book simply because it is my favorite short bike ride. Runnymede Road, though only a little over a mile in length, is a real gem—flat, windy, narrow, and treed, with some nice stone ruins along its course. It's so nice that this ride traverses it twice. Saint Malachi Church, at the crest of St. Malachi Road, affords expansive views of the surrounding countryside. The church has been there for more than 150 years, and outside of Philadelphia, it is the oldest Catholic mission church still used for worship in southeastern Pennsylvania. The large horse breeding farms here keep the scenery spectacularly open with miles-long views in all directions.

When you start up Thouron Road, you will see immense horse-grazing pastures on both sides and will notice an estate with some green-

1. Runnymede Road – Saint Malachi Church

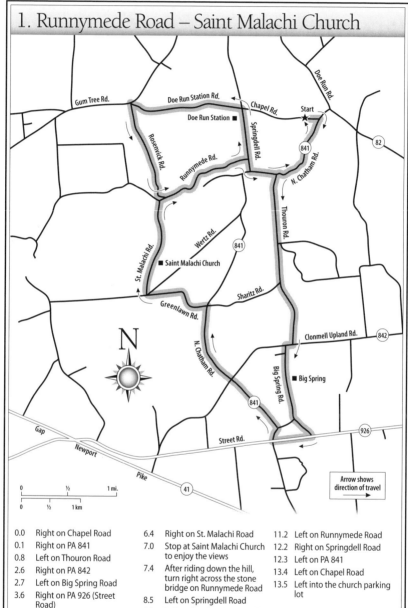

0.0	Right on Chapel Road	
0.1	Right on PA 841	
0.8	Left on Thouron Road	
2.6	Right on PA 842	
2.7	Left on Big Spring Road	
3.6	Right on PA 926 (Street Road)	
4.0	Right on PA 841	
5.7	Left on Greenlawn Road and ride up the hill	
6.4	Right on St. Malachi Road	
7.0	Stop at Saint Malachi Church to enjoy the views	
7.4	After riding down the hill, turn right across the stone bridge on Runnymede Road	
8.5	Left on Springdell Road	
9.0	Left on Doe Run Station Rd	
10.2	Left on Rosenvick Road and ride down a hill to Runnymede Road	
11.2	Left on Runnymede Road	
12.2	Right on Springdell Road	
12.3	Left on PA 841	
13.4	Left on Chapel Road	
13.5	Left into the church parking lot	

houses on your left. This is Doe Run, the 220-acre estate of the late Sir John Rupert Hunt Thouron and the late Lady Thouron. Christie's currently has it on the market for $15 million if you're interested. Besides being a renowned thoroughbred farm, it is a horticultural landmark because of its exquisite gardens. Lady Thouron, born of the du Pont family, was the original donor behind the New Bolton Center of the University of Pennsylvania. Google "Sir John Thouron" and read about his remarkable life. In addition to his many eleemosynary activities, he was a widely respected horticulturist. He volunteered for service in World War II, training commandos for the British Army and parachuting many times behind enemy lines.

Especially if you are riding on a warm day, stop at Big Spring and enjoy the cool shade. The spring is on private land, which should be respected. It is of modest dimensions, marked only by a few boards driven into the moist earth and surrounded by watercress and skunk cabbage. The force of the upwelling water is a sight to behold, however.

0.0 Turn right on Chapel Road.

0.1 Turn right on PA 841.

0.8 Turn left on Thouron Road.

Watch the open-grate metal bridge just before this turn. This is where the rough pavement begins and continues for 2.7 miles. There are no significant hills, and if you ride slowly you will find it worthwhile.

2.6 Turn right on PA 842.

2.7 Turn left on Big Spring Road.

The pavement on this stretch is also rough and is included in the 2.7-mile total previously described. At about 3.2 miles, stop, walk to the left side of the road, and look in the deep shade for the eponymous Big Spring bubbling up in the watercress and lush greenery. This is a real oasis on a hot summer day.

3.6 Turn right on PA 926 (Street Road).

4.0 Turn right on PA 841.

5.7 Turn left on Greenlawn Road and ride up the hill.

6.4 Turn right on St. Malachi Road.

Runnymede Road

Be sure not to take the sharp right on Wertz Road. St. Malachi Road is a right-angle turn.

7.0 Stop at Saint Malachi Church to enjoy the views.
Saint Malachi is an active Roman Catholic church that holds Sunday services.

7.4 After riding down the hill, turn right across the stone bridge on Runnymede Road.
Pause at the bridge; this is a lovely spot and the beginning of one of the nicest bicycle roads anywhere.

8.5 Turn left on Springdell Road.

9.0 Turn left on Doe Run Station Road.

10.2 Turn left on Rosenvick Road and ride down a hill to Runnymede Road.

11.2 Turn left on Runnymede Road.
It's so nice; why not do it again?

12.2 Turn right on Springdell Road.

12.3 Turn left on PA 841.

On the near right corner of this intersection is an English-style pub called The Whip Tavern, which is worth a stop after finishing this ride. Be cautious again crossing the open-grate bridge after passing Thouron Road on the right.

13.4 Turn left on Chapel Road.

13.5 Turn left into the church parking lot where this ride began.

2. Stargazer's Stone

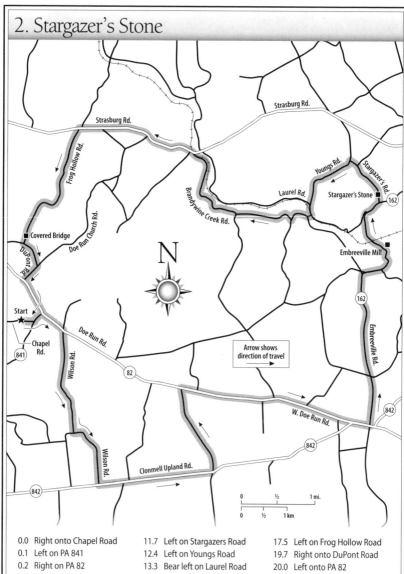

Arrow shows direction of travel
→

0.0 Right onto Chapel Road	11.7 Left on Stargazers Road	17.5 Left on Frog Hollow Road
0.1 Left on PA 841	12.4 Left on Youngs Road	19.7 Right onto DuPont Road
0.2 Right on PA 82	13.3 Bear left on Laurel Road	20.0 Left onto PA 82
0.6 Right on Wilson Road	13.4 Right across the bridge and bear right on Brandywine Creek Road	20.4 Right on PA 841
1.9 Left to stay on Wilson Road		20.6 Right on Chapel Road
2.8 Left on PA 842	13.7 Right to continue on Brandywine Creek Road	20.7 Left into church parking lot
4.4 Left on Newark Road		
5.6 Right on PA 82	15.8 Left on Strasburg Road (PA 162)	
8.2 Left on PA 162 (Embreeville-Unionville Road)		

Paul Woodward, © The Countryman Press

Stargazer's Stone

- **DISTANCE:** 20.7 miles
- **TERRAIN/DIFFICULTY:** Rolling hills; easy
- **START:** Parking lot of Chapel Road Baptist Church on Chapel Road in Doe Run
- **GPS COORDINATES OF START:** N39 54.863' / W75 49.332'
- **GETTING THERE/PARKING:** Take PA 82 to Doe Run and turn on PA 841, which intersects PA 82 from the south and ends there. Take the first right turn on Chapel Road and look for the church on the left side at 0.1 mile. Please do not park here during Sunday services.
- **HIGHLIGHTS:** Stargazer's Stone, Embreeville Mill, covered bridge, Brandywine Creek, horse farms

Besides being a pleasant ride in beautiful countryside, this excursion provides much of historical interest. On private property about 0.1 mile north of Embreeville Road on Stargazers Road on the right side is Stargazer's Stone, and a rider could easily pass it without realizing its significance. The Mason-Dixon Line was surveyed between 1763 and 1767 by astronomer Charles Mason and surveyor Jeremiah Dixon to resolve a boundary dispute between the Calvert family of Maryland and the Penn family of Pennsylvania. The resulting lines, one east–west, the other north–south, demarcated the borders of four states: Pennsylvania, Maryland, Delaware, and West Virginia. Stargazer's Stone served as an astronomical observation point for the survey when this portion of the Mason-Dixon Line was laid out in 1764, and the line lies 15 miles south of the stone. The John Harland farmhouse, at the junction of PA 162 and Stargazers Road, already stood on that site during the survey.

This ride in the Upper Brandywine Valley crosses a covered bridge and passes a centuries-old mill that is still active as a feed store. It starts at the same point as ride 1 and can easily be combined with it. The first part on Wilson and Newark roads passes through some huge horse farms with great views. The second part goes through Embreeville on the Brandywine River and past Stargazer's Stone. The last part stays close to the upper Brandywine River and then descends shaded Frog Hollow Road over a small covered bridge and back to the start.

0.0 Turn right out of the lot onto Chapel Road.

0.1 Turn left on PA 841.

0.2 Turn right on PA 82.

0.6 Turn right on Wilson Road.

1.9 Turn left to stay on Wilson Road.
The sign says Ryan Road, but Wilson continues to the left.

2.8 Turn left on PA 842.

4.4 Turn left on Newark Road.

5.6 Turn right on PA 82.

8.2 Turn left on PA 162 (Embreeville-Unionville Road).
There is a sign that says WOLLASTON ROAD, but the road to the left is PA 162. A beautiful bridge crosses Brandywine Creek near 10.7 miles, and just beyond it is the Embreeville Mill.

11.7 Turn left on Stargazers Road.
The old house on the corner is the Harland House. Watch for the small stone structure on a knoll on the right side at 11.8 miles. That is Stargazer's Stone. It is on private land and not accessible to the public.

12.4 Turn left on Youngs Road.

13.3 Bear left on Laurel Road.

Embreeville Mill

There is no sign here.

13.4 Turn right across the bridge and bear right on Brandywine Creek Road.

13.7 Turn right to continue on Brandywine Creek Road.
Always stay on the main road and don't take any left turns until reaching Strasburg Road.

15.8 Turn left on Strasburg Road (PA 162).

17.5 Turn left on Frog Hollow Road.
Some maps name this Hephzibah Doe Run Road; there is no sign. At 19.3 miles cross a covered bridge (Speakman Bridge number 1) and bear left; this is Covered Bridge Road.

19.7 Turn right onto DuPont Road.

20.0 Turn left onto PA 82.

20.4 Turn right on PA 841.

20.6 Turn right on Chapel Road.

20.7 Turn left into the church parking lot.

3. Apple Grove Road — King Ranch Land

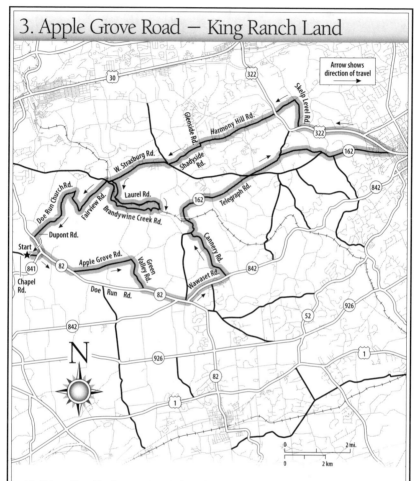

Apple Grove Road—
King Ranch Land

- **DISTANCE:** 36.6 miles
- **TERRAIN/DIFFICULTY:** Rolling hills with a couple of climbs; moderate
- **START:** Parking lot of Chapel Road Baptist Church in Doe Run
- **GPS COORDINATES OF START:** N39 54.863' / W75 49.332'
- **GETTING THERE/PARKING:** Take PA 82 and turn on PA 841, which intersects PA 82 from the south and ends there. Take the first right turn on Chapel Road and look for the church on the left side at 0.1 mile. Please do not park here during Sunday services.
- **HIGHLIGHTS:** Old King Ranch Land, covered bridge, fox hunting in season

This ride goes through some of the most splendid horse country in Chester County. Miles of white board fencing surround huge grazing pastures where elite horseflesh is part of the scenery.

On weekends between October and February, bicyclists may hear the hunter's horn and be lucky to see the great spectacle of a fox hunt. The Masters of Foxhounds Association, established in 1907, sets the stringent rules for these hunts, in which the emphasis is on the chase rather than the kill. On the vast majority of these hunts, the hounds lose the scent and the fox is never actually pursued. When they do find the spoor, the chase is on: 15 to 20 pairs of specially bred and trained hounds bay as they run through the fields in pursuit. They are followed by a large group of formally dressed, red-coated riders on fine mounts. The chase ends when the fox goes into a hole in the ground called an earth. The hounds are then rewarded for their efforts, and the fox gets away. In some areas, coyotes are hunted rather than fox. It is a thrill to witness one of these hunts in this beautiful countryside.

This is the longest and most strenuous ride in this book. It is a ride of contrasts, starting in horse country and then passing close to some of the more populated areas of central Chester County. At 21.6 miles it crosses a covered bridge. After entering the Upper Brandywine River Valley and following that stream for a few miles, it reenters horse country before returning you to the start.

0.0 Turn right on Chapel Road.

0.1 Turn left on PA 841.

0.2 Turn right on PA 82.

1.4 Turn left on Apple Grove Road.

3.2 Turn right on Green Valley Road.

4.2 Turn left on PA 82.

5.7 Turn left on PA 842 (Wawasset-Unionville Road).

7.2 Turn left on Cannery Road.

9.0 Turn right on PA 162.

13.8 Continue straight on Telegraph Road.
This segment changes its name from Embreeville to Glen Hall, and then to Telegraph Road. There is a stretch of rough pavement between 14.0 and 14.7 miles.

14.7 Turn left on PA 162.

17.0 Turn left on US 322 in West Chester.
Although there is some traffic on this road, there is a good shoulder.

20.1 Turn right on Skelp Level Road and ride up the hill.
This is a pretty strenuous ride, and Skelp Level Road is anything but level.

21.0 Turn left on Harmony Hill Road.

21.6 Cross a covered bridge.

A young bicyclist checks out the thoroughbreds on Apple Grove Road.

21.7 Cross US 322 and stay on Harmony Hill Road.
Some maps call this road Shadyside as soon as it crosses US 322.

24.2 Turn left on Glenside Road.

24.3 Turn right on Shadyside Road.

25.3 Turn right on Strasburg Road (PA 162).

27.3 Turn left Laurel Road.
This is called Creek Road on some maps.

29.3 Bear right to remain on Laurel Road.

29.4 Turn right across the bridge.

29.5 Turn right on Brandywine Creek Road and continue on it until Strasburg Road.
All the roads leading off to the left on this stretch have been closed due to conservation easements. They are all dead-end roads.

31.9 Turn left on Strasburg Road, and then take an immediate left turn on Fairview Road.

33.1 Turn right on Hephzibah Doe Run Church Road.

33.8 Turn left on Doe Run Church Road.
There is a short stretch of rough pavement between 35.1 and 35.5 miles.

35.6 Continue straight on DuPont Road.

35.8 Turn left on PA 82.

36.3 Turn right on PA 841.

36.5 Turn right on Chapel Road.

36.6 Turn left into the chapel parking lot.

BRANDYWINE VALLEY

Jefferis Bridge

RIDING IN THE UPPER BRANDYWINE RIVER VALLEY can be confusing, because there are two main branches (east and west), numerous small tributaries, and the main watercourse itself, which flows through Wilmington, Delaware, and then into the Christina River, from which it empties into the Delaware River. The two main branches join in Chester County just north of Lenape and south of Jefferis Bridge, which spans the West Branch. There are several roads called "Creek" or "Brandywine Creek" in the upper valley, so keep this in mind as you go exploring. This is very pretty country, and much of the upper river and many historic structures have been preserved.

The Brandywine Battlefield covers an area of about 10 square miles in the Upper Brandywine Valley, where on September 11, 1777, fifteen thousand British and Hessian troops under Lieutenant-General Howe met an approximately equal force of soldiers of the Continental Army under the command of George Washington. Howe had landed his force at Head of Elk in the upper Chesapeake Bay and advanced through Delaware to camp in Kennett Square, where he intended to rest his troops before pushing on to capture Philadelphia. Between him and that capital city, Washington had arrayed his army to guard the fords and high ground on the east side of Brandywine Creek. He expected Howe's main attack to occur at Chadds Ford, which was on the main road from Baltimore to Philadelphia.

Howe had superior knowledge of the terrain, which he had acquired from Loyalists in the area, and planned a flanking maneuver that the British had used so successfully against the Continentals in the Battle of Long Island the previous March. He split his force and sent seven thousand of his troops in the early-morning fog to challenge and confuse the Continentals at Chadds Ford. Meanwhile, he took his eight-thousand-strong main force north to cross the unguarded fords there. By early afternoon, he had safely brought his entire flanking force across the river 8 miles north of Chadds Ford and attacked the Continentals' right flank. The main battle occurred later in the afternoon on Battle Hill near Birmingham Friends Meetinghouse. At the end of the day, the Continentals were driven from the field and retreated to Chester. The British captured Philadelphia on September 26th.

The four rides in this section—rides 4, 5, 6, and 7—will give you a good taste of this beautiful area and provide access to a number of museums, such as the Brandywine River Museum, Delaware Museum of Natural History, Winterthur Museum, and Hagley Museum. Ride 7 allows you to explore the battlefield and ride along the river, while ride 4 starts in the parking lot of Longwood Gardens and loops into the countryside to the north. Ride 5, which also starts at Longwood, follows scenic DE 52 southward toward Wilmington and then turns northward back into Pennsylvania along the Brandywine River on DE 100. Ride 6 begins near the polo fields south of Toughkenamon, Pennsylvania, and goes cross country, cutting into the "dome" of Delaware and turning around in Chadds Ford.

Tourism Information

There is a large assortment of chain hotels in this area.

www.chaddsford.com

www.chaddsfordhistory.org

www.longwoodgardens.org

www.winterthur.org

www.brandywineconservancy.org

Bicycle Shops

Bike Line of Wilmington, 2900 North Concord Pike, Wilmington; 302-478-9438

For more bicycle shops, see the West Chester section.

4

Longwood North

- **DISTANCE:** 16.9 miles
- **TERRAIN/DIFFICULTY:** Rolling hills; easy
- **START:** Longwood Gardens parking lot
- **GPS COORDINATES OF START:** N39 52.215' / W75 40.338'
- **GETTING THERE/PARKING:** Take the Longwood Gardens exit from US 1 and follow the signs into the parking lot
- **HIGHLIGHTS:** Longwood Gardens, open countryside

This is a nice ride through some beautiful countryside, but the main attraction is Longwood Gardens, America's premier display garden. There are 1,050 acres of gardens displaying more than 11,000 types of plants organized into 20 outdoor gardens, 20 indoor gardens, and a 4-acre conservatory building. It is open every day year-round, and there are numerous special programs, displays, and concerts to enjoy. The fireworks-and-fountains concerts in the summer months are not to be missed. The smoke and colors of the fireworks mix with the mist of the illuminated fountains, all choreographed to classical music like Saint-Saëns's *Organ Symphony*. From November to January the gardens are illuminated with Christmas lights the like of which you have probably never seen. You would feel well rewarded for any time you set aside to visit this remarkable place.

The gardens have a long and interesting history, starting with the purchase of the land by George Peirce, a Quaker, in 1700. The Peirce family farmed the land until 1798, when Joshua and Samuel Peirce planted the first specimens of an arboretum. By 1850 they had managed to grow one of the finest collections of trees in the United States.

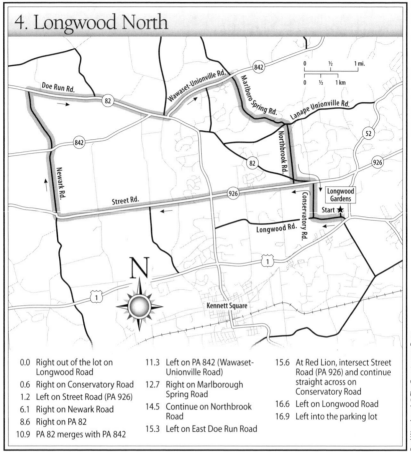

4. Longwood North

0.0	Right out of the lot on Longwood Road	
0.6	Right on Conservatory Road	
1.2	Left on Street Road (PA 926)	
6.1	Right on Newark Road	
8.6	Right on PA 82	
10.9	PA 82 merges with PA 842	
11.3	Left on PA 842 (Wawaset-Unionville Road)	
12.7	Right on Marlborough Spring Road	
14.5	Continue on Northbrook Road	
15.3	Left on East Doe Run Road	
15.6	At Red Lion, intersect Street Road (PA 926) and continue straight across on Conservatory Road	
16.6	Left on Longwood Road	
16.9	Left into the parking lot	

The great industrialist Pierre S. du Pont purchased it in 1906 to keep it from being sold for lumber. He built his residence on the land, and over the ensuing 30 years, with his wife, Alice Belin du Pont, he set about transforming the derelict arboretum into what you see today. Some of the original trees can still be seen on the grounds. In 1937 Pierre du Pont created the Longwood Foundation to care for the gardens and ensure access to the public in perpetuity.

Pierre du Pont was the great-grandson of E. I. du Pont, the founder of the DuPont Company (E. I. du Pont de Nemours and Company, headquartered in Wilmington, Delaware). He graduated from MIT in 1890 with a degree in chemistry and entered the world of business, where he became what today might be called a "turnaround specialist." In 1902, with two of his cousins, he purchased the then-troubled DuPont Company, turning it into a major American corporation. At the same time he was chairman of the board of that company he also held the same office for General Motors, where he spearheaded its progress from near bankruptcy to the world's largest corporation. His other interests in education, horticulture, transportation, and preservation have altered the cultural and physical landscape of Delaware and southeastern Pennsylvania.

This ride is a loop that allows you to explore some of the Upper Brandywine Valley north of Longwood.

0.0 Turn right out of the lot on Longwood Road.

0.6 Turn right on Conservatory Road.

1.2 Turn left on Street Road (PA 926).

6.1 Turn right on Newark Road.

Entrance to Longwood Gardens

8.6 Turn right on PA 82.

10.9 PA 82 merges with PA 842.

11.3 Turn left on PA 842 (Wawaset-Unionville Road).

12.7 Turn right on Marlborough Spring Road.

14.5 Continue on Northbrook Road.

15.3 Turn left on East Doe Run Road.

15.6 At Red Lion, intersect Street Road (PA 926) and continue straight across on Conservatory Road.

16.6 Turn left on Longwood Road.

16.9 Turn left into the parking lot.

5

Longwood South into Delaware

- **DISTANCE:** 22.5 miles; 27.4 miles following alternate route
- **TERRAIN/DIFFICULTY:** Rolling hills, mostly flat; easy
- **START:** Longwood Gardens parking lot
- **GPS COORDINATES OF START:** N39 52.215' / W75 40.338'
- **GETTING THERE/PARKING:** Take the Longwood Gardens exit from US 1 and follow the signs into the parking lot
- **HIGHLIGHTS:** Longwood Gardens, Brandywine River, Delaware "chateau country," Delaware Museum of Natural History, Winterthur, Hagley Museum

This ride is best scheduled for Saturday or Sunday morning, when traffic is lighter, or on weekdays 10–3. DE 52 is a pleasure to ride and has a nice, wide, smooth shoulder. Along the way bicyclists will pass the Delaware Museum of Natural History, renowned for its excellent collection of seashells, and Winterthur, a former du Pont estate with a world-renowned collection of American antiques and beautiful grounds resplendent with flowering shrubs in the springtime. Hagley Museum, exhibiting examples of early American industry, is near the intersection of Barley Mill and Montchanin roads. DE 100 follows the Brandywine River as it goes north through Delaware's "chateau country." At the north end of the concrete bridge across the Brandywine River, on the east side of the road, is a gate. This is the starting point for the Point-to-Point antique-carriage procession, held the first Sunday afternoon in May. It is a memorable spectacle.

At the end of Station Way Road, immediately south of US 1 in Chadds Ford, stands the Brandywine River Museum, home of a splen-

5. Longwood South into Delaware

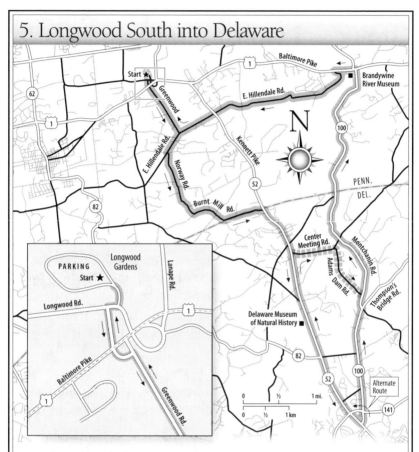

0.0 Right out of the parking lot on Longwood Road

0.1 Left on Greenwood Road

0.2 Cross US 1 and continue on Greenwood Road, which curves to the left

0.3 Right to continue on Greenwood Road

1.3 Right on Hillendale Road

1.7 Left on Norway Road

2.5 Bear right to remain on Norway Road

3.1 Left on Burnt Mill Road

4.7 Right on Kennett Pike (DE 52 South)

9.4 Left on Montchanin Road (DE 100 North)

11.7 Bear left on Montchanin Road

16.8 Left on Station Way Road. Ride through the Brandywine River Museum parking lot and walk over the bridge on US 1 toward the south

17.1 Left on Fairville Road.

21.2 Right on Greenwood Road

22.2 Left to continue on Greenwood Road to the light on US 1

22.3 Cross US 1 at the light

22.4 Right on Longwood Road

22.5 Enter the parking lot

Alternate route (from mile 9.4):

9.6 Left on Barley Mill Road

9.9 Right on DE 52

14.2 Right on Center Meeting Road

15.5 Right on Adams Dam Road

16.7 Left on DE 100

21.6 Left on Station Way Road and follow the ride directions to Fairville Road (as described in mile 17.1 of the original route)

26.0 Right on Greenwood Road

27.1 Left to continue on Greenwood Road to US 1

27.2 Cross US 1 at the light

27.3 Right on Longwood Road

27.4 Left into the parking lot

Paul Woodward, © The Countryman Press

did collection of paintings by members of the Wyeth family. After the ride, make it a point to visit one or more of these landmarks.

The national land preservation group Last Chance Landscapes has designated DE 52 as one of the 12 most endangered scenic roadways in the nation. Local associations have succeeded in having the Kennett Pike, as it is also known, designated as a greenway, a natural area for wildlife and human-powered transportation. The original roadway was laid out between 1811 and 1813 as a toll road and was 7 miles long. Of the two original toll houses, one still stands on the grounds of Winterthur Museum. Tolls were collected on the basis of livestock being driven or on carriage size and number of passengers. Travelers to funerals and church services were allowed free passage.

In 1919 Pierre S. du Pont purchased the road for $60,000 and invested $125,000 to have it paved from the Pennsylvania state line to Wilmington. It is rumored that he paved the road to facilitate his trip from his home in Longwood to the DuPont Company headquarters in Wilmington. The next year he sold it back to the state for one dollar with three stipulations: that there be no rails or trolleys, that there be no billboards or advertising signs, and that a certain historic pear tree be preserved. The historic tree, by the way, managed to survive until 1979, when it was hit by a truck and died. Daily traffic volume on DE 52 has actually decreased since 1900.

The segments of DE 100 north of Barley Mill Road are also called Montchanin Road, Creek Road, and Chadds Ford Road, in that order from south to north. Although the road does not have a shoulder, it is nice to ride during off-peak traffic hours. During the bike ride, from about 15 miles on, PA 100 stays close to the Brandywine River.

0.0 Turn right out of the parking lot on Longwood Road.

0.1 Turn left on Greenwood Road.

0.2 Cross US 1 and continue on Greenwood Road, which curves to the left.

0.3 Turn right to continue on Greenwood Road.

1.3 Turn right on Hillendale Road.

1.7 Turn left on Norway Road.

2.5 Bear right to remain on Norway Road.

3.1 Turn left on Burnt Mill Road.

4.7 Turn right on Kennett Pike (DE 52 South).
You are now in Delaware. The entrance to Winterthur is on the left at 6.8 miles. You'll pass the Delaware Museum of Natural History, on the right, at 7.3 miles.

9.4 Turn left on Montchanin Road (DE 100 North).
DE 100 does not have a shoulder and can have a lot of traffic during rush hour and on weekend afternoons. It follows the Brandywine River to Chadds Ford and traverses much pretty countryside.

11.7 Bear left on Montchanin Road.

16.8 Turn left on Station Way Road. Ride through the parking lot of the Brandy-wine River Museum and walk over the bridge on US 1 toward the south.
Stay on the left side, facing traffic; the bridge is less than 100 yards long.

17.1 Turn left on Fairville Road.
There is a traffic light on US 1 that allows a safe turn onto Fairville Road, or bikes can be walked through a parking lot on the left just before the light. Fairville Road becomes Hillendale Road when it crosses the railroad tracks at 18.1 miles.

21.2 Turn right on Greenwood Road.

22.2 Turn left to continue on Greenwood Road to the light on US 1.

22.3 Cross US 1 at the light.

22.4 Turn right on Longwood Road.

22.5 Enter the parking lot.

If you happen to get on DE 100 North during a time of heavy traffic and you are uncomfortable riding this stretch, there is a bailout after mile 9.4:

9.6 Turn left on Barley Mill Road.
The entrance to the Hagley Museum is to the right. This is the first intersection north of the turn onto DE 100 from DE 52.

9.9 Turn right on DE 52.

The Point-to-Point antique-carriage procession, held each May, is a sight to see.

14.2 Turn right on Center Meeting Road.

15.5 Turn right on Adams Dam Road.

16.7 Turn left on DE 100.

21.6 Turn left on Station Way Road and follow the ride directions back to Fairville Road (as described in mile 17.1 of the original route).

26.0 Turn right on Greenwood Road.

27.1 Turn left to continue on Greenwood Road to US 1.

27.2 Cross US 1 at the light.

27.3 Turn right on Longwood Road.

27.4 Turn left into the parking lot.

6

Hillendale Road

- **DISTANCE:** 21.1 miles
- **TERRAIN/DIFFICULTY:** Rolling hills; easy
- **START:** Parking lot of the New Garden Elementary School
- **GPS COORDINATES OF START:** N39 48.592' / W75 44.806'
- **GETTING THERE/PARKING:** From PA 41, turn on New Garden Road. This road is a loop and intersects PA 41 twice within a mile; it is on the northeast side of PA 41. You want the more southerly intersection just south of the Newark Road intersection. The school is on the right in 0.1 mile.
- **HIGHLIGHTS:** Nice, long country road; Brandywine Polo Club fields; New Garden Flying Field

The aptly named Hillendale Road provides a long stretch of rolling country road and beautiful scenery. The Brandywine Polo Club fields are located near here, at 260 Polo Road, about a mile north of Hillendale Road on Newark Road next to the New Garden Flying Field. The club's Web site, www.brandywinepoloclub.com, has schedules for the matches, so you may be able to plan a ride to allow time to see this unusual and spectacular sport. (A Sunday ride returning you to the start by 3 PM—the time at which most of the matches begin between June and the end of September—is a good bet.)

In the game of polo, each team fields four riders and their mounts, and the object is to strike a small, hard ball with a long-handled mallet through the opposing team's goal. The game is played at a brisk pace, and horses are traded out when they are tired—each rider has a string of between two and six ponies, depending upon the length of the

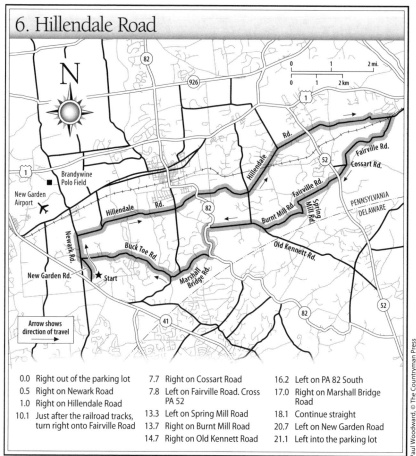

6. Hillendale Road

Mile	Direction	Mile	Direction	Mile	Direction
0.0	Right out of the parking lot	7.7	Right on Cossart Road	16.2	Left on PA 82 South
0.5	Right on Newark Road	7.8	Left on Fairville Road. Cross PA 52	17.0	Right on Marshall Bridge Road
1.0	Right on Hillendale Road	13.3	Left on Spring Mill Road	18.1	Continue straight
10.1	Just after the railroad tracks, turn right onto Fairville Road	13.7	Right on Burnt Mill Road	20.7	Left on New Garden Road
		14.7	Right on Old Kennett Road	21.1	Left into the parking lot

Paul Woodward, © The Countryman Press

match. While they are referred to as "ponies," they are actually full-sized horses, usually Thoroughbreds or Thoroughbred crosses that are specially selected for speed, agility, and temperament. These horses undergo lengthy training regimens and can have careers as long as 15 years.

Along with polo fields, this ride also features the Flying Field, but instead of polo ponies, this field is home to many stunt pilots, whom you may see performing aerobatic maneuvers overhead in classic Stearman biplanes. The airport is home to the Colonial Flying Corps Museum, which sponsors an annual air show in June.

The ride itself is basically a long cruise from west to east and turns

Mown field along Hillendale Road

back just short of Chadds Ford. The return loop to the south of Hillendale Road meanders westward on back roads and stays just north of the Delaware border.

0.0 Turn right out of the school parking lot on New Garden Road.

0.5 Turn right on Newark Road.

1.0 Turn right on Hillendale Road.
Follow Hillendale all the way across PA 52 toward Chadds Ford.

10.1 Just after the railroad tracks, turn right onto Fairville Road.
This can be confusing, because this road changes names several times back and forth between Fairville and Stockford roads. Continue straight and avoid left turns.

11.7 Turn right on Cossart Road.

11.8 Turn left on Fairville Road. Cross PA 52.
After it crosses PA 52, Fairville continues as South Fairville Road.

13.3 Turn left on Spring Mill Road.

13.7 Turn right on Burnt Mill Road.

14.7 Turn right on Old Kennett Road.

16.2 Turn left on PA 82 South.

17.0 Turn right on Marshall Bridge Road.

18.1 Continue straight.

This road changes names to Kaolin, Chandler Mill, and Buck Toe roads, and the signage is poor. Its final incarnation is Buck Toe Road when it intersects Newark Road.

20.7 Turn left on New Garden Road.

21.1 Turn left into the school parking lot.

7. Brandywine Battlefield

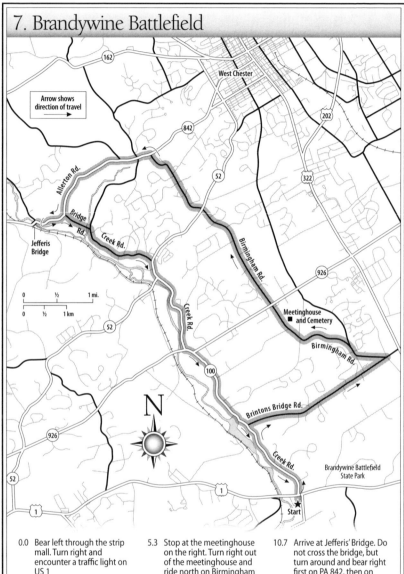

0.0 Bear left through the strip mall. Turn right and encounter a traffic light on US 1

0.1 Cross US 1 and continue on PA 100 (Creek Road)

1.4 Right on Brintons Bridge Road and ride up the hill

3.6 Left on Birmingham Road

5.3 Stop at the meetinghouse on the right. Turn right out of the meetinghouse and ride north on Birmingham Road

8.6 Left on PA 842

8.7 Bear right on Allerton Road

10.7 Arrive at Jefferis' Bridge. Do not cross the bridge, but turn around and bear right first on PA 842, then on Creek Road (PA 100). Continue on Creek Road

17.2 Cross US 1 at the traffic light and turn back into the mall parking lot

17.3 Arrive back at the post office parking lot

Paul Woodward, © The Countryman Press

7

Brandywine Battlefield

- **DISTANCE:** 17.3 miles
- **TERRAIN/DIFFICULTY:** Mostly flat, with some rolling hills and one long hill; easy to moderate
- **START:** Parking lot of Chadds Ford Post Office
- **GPS COORDINATES OF START:** N39 52.276' / W75 35.430'
- **GETTING THERE/PARKING:** From US 1, turn south on PA 100 and immediately turn into the post office parking lot; there is a large unpaved lot behind the building
- **HIGHLIGHTS:** Revolutionary War battlefield, Brandywine River Museum, Birmingham Meetinghouse and cemetery, scenery of the Upper Brandywine Valley

This ride will follow the course of the 1777 battle in reverse. Starting in Chadds Ford, you will ride north along the creek and turn northeast on Brintons Bridge Road, climbing the long hill out of the river valley to the high ground near the meetinghouse. As you work your way up the hill, you are roughly retracing the rapid march of Washington's soldiers, who covered the 4 miles in 45 minutes after it had been discovered that the British attack on Chadds Ford was a diversion. The day had turned very hot and sunny after the morning fog had burned off, and these men made this climb wearing uniforms and carrying weapons and ammunition.

At the top of the climb you will turn left and ride to the meetinghouse, which was used as a hospital for the wounded at the time of the battle, and to the cemetery, which was the site of a battlefield. Take some time to read the monuments in the southern part of the ceme-

Horse farm, Upper Brandywine Valley

tery. Riding down the long hill from there, you will be facing the British line of attack. When you turn left on PA 842, the ride will take you back to the river, where you will be able to see Jefferis Bridge, which stands on the site of the ford that the British used to cross the creek.

From that point you can cruise back south along the river on PA 100 until you return to US 1 and the start.

0.0 In the post office parking lot, facing north, ride past the post office and bear left through the small strip mall. Turn right on the road there and immediately encounter a traffic light on US 1.

0.1 Cross US 1 through the light and continue on PA 100 (Creek Road).

1.4 Turn right on Brintons Bridge Road and ride up the hill.

As you pause to make the right turn, look left toward the river, and you will see the home and studio of the late artist Andrew Wyeth.

3.6 Turn left on Birmingham Road.

The historic Dilworthtown Inn is located on the far left side of this intersection.

5.3 Stop at the Birmingham Friends Meeting House on the right. Turn right out of the meetinghouse and ride north on Birmingham Road.

The adjacent Birmingham Lafayette Cemetery contains numerous commemorative monuments and is worth a visit.

8.6 Turn left on PA 842.

8.7 Bear right on Allerton Road.

10.7 Arrive at Jefferis Bridge. Do not cross the bridge, but turn around and bear right first on PA 842, then on Creek Road (PA 100). Continue on Creek Road.

The site of the bridge was an unguarded ford at the time of the battle and the place at which the British crossed the river to outflank the Continentals.

17.2 Cross US 1 at the traffic light and turn back into the mall parking lot.

17.3 Arrive back at the post office parking lot.

WEST CHESTER

Greek Revival–style house, West Chester

THE BOROUGH OF WEST CHESTER is located near the intersections of US 202, US 322, and PA 100 and has been the seat of government of Chester County since 1786. Originally settled by Quakers early in the 18th century, it has grown into a lively commercial center of about eighteen thousand people. The Greek Revival–style architecture of the downtown is worth seeing, as is the campus of West Chester University.

This is a good location from which to explore the countryside of the eastern part of the county. Rides 8 and 9 share a start in the parking lot of Bradford Plaza in West Chester. Ride 8 goes west into the Upper Brandywine River Valley and travels through farm country. Ride 9 starts on the streets of the borough and travels through the eastern suburbs to the gate of the Westtown School before it turns back into town. This is the farthest east any of these rides will take you because both the population density and traffic increase to the north and east, compromising the quality of the bicycling experience.

Tourism Information

The West Chester area has the usual assortment of chain hotels and restaurants.

www.downtownwestchester.com

www.westchesterdish.com

Bicycle Shops

Bike Line, 700 Lawrence Drive, West Chester; 610-429-4370

Hotfoot Cycles, 319 West Gay Street, West Chester; 610-719-4977

West Chester Bicycle Center, 1342 West Chester Pike, West Chester; 610-431-1856

8

Ground Hog College Road

- **DISTANCE:** 17.4 miles
- **TERRAIN/DIFFICULTY:** Rolling hills, short section of rough pavement; easy
- **START:** Parking lot of Bradford Plaza shopping center in West Chester
- **GPS COORDINATES OF START:** N39 57.601' / W75 37.242'
- **GETTING THERE/PARKING:** From US 202/322, take the PA 3 exit and drive straight through West Chester until you reach the intersection of PA 162 and PA 322. Bradford Plaza is just beyond this intersection on the right side on PA 162.
- **HIGHLIGHTS:** Upper Brandywine Valley

This ride begins on the west side of West Chester and goes west into the Upper Brandywine River Valley. It's hard to find a better road name in English than Ground Hog College Road; I have not been able to determine its origins.

As you ride through this beautiful countryside, you may notice that the landscape has been formed by the hand of man. The human hand has lain on this land for centuries, and yet, for the most part, the scenery has not suffered because of it. It is not an untrammeled natural landscape like Yosemite Valley but very much tamed and formed by human activity, yet it is beautiful. Some areas of the county have been ruined and restored; some have been preserved. Lancaster and Chester counties look the way they do because people have cared about them for a long time. Absent this stewardship, most of this countryside would be strip malls and tract housing. The Amish have created a har-

8. Ground Hog College Road

0.0	Right on PA 162 (Strasburg Road)	
5.3	Left on Ground Hog College Road, which becomes Warpath Road	
6.8	Right on Brandywine Road	
8.3	Right on PA 162	
9.3	Right on Broad Run Road	
10.9	Left on Northbrook Road	
12.3	Right on PA 162	
12.8	Right on Lucky Hill Road	
14.9	Left on Allerton Road, cross Jefferis' Bridge, and continue straight on PA 842	
16.8	Left on South Bradford Avenue	
17.3	Left at the light and immediately turn right into the Bradford Plaza lot	
17.4	Arrive at start	

Paul Woodward, © The Countryman Press

monious agrarian landscape, and a concentration of wealthy individuals has done the rest, preserving large tracts of land in the county either as horse and cattle farms, or as nature preserves for the benefit of posterity.

A recent example is the opening in August 2007 of ChesLen Preserve, a 1,263-acre tract of land containing 2 miles of the banks of the West Branch of the Brandywine River between Embreeville and Unionville. It was once part of the 17,000-acre King Ranch lands and is the gift of a private philanthropist combined with a large parcel of county land. (You will ride past it on rides 2, 3, and 4.) This is why this countryside looks the way it does. It did not happen by accident.

Downtown West Chester

This ride is a loop that begins as a nice long stretch on Strasburg Road, then turns south into the forests along the Brandywine headwaters. The forest gives way to some farmland, through which you ride back into West Chester.

0.0 Turn right on PA 162 (Strasburg Road).

5.3 Turn left on Ground Hog College Road, which becomes Warpath Road.

6.8 Turn right on Brandywine Road.

8.3 Turn right on PA 162.

9.3 Turn right on Broad Run Road.
Between 9.3 and 9.6 miles the pavement is broken with some loose gravel on top. This road is shady and runs along the creek. The pavement becomes smooth again at 9.6 miles.

10.9 Turn left on Northbrook Road.

12.3 Turn right on PA 162.

12.8 Turn right on Lucky Hill Road.

14.9 Turn left on Allerton Road, cross Jefferis Bridge, and continue straight on PA 842.

16.8 Turn left on South Bradford Avenue.

17.3 Turn left at the light and immediately turn right into the Bradford Plaza lot.

17.4 Arrive at start.

9. Westtown School

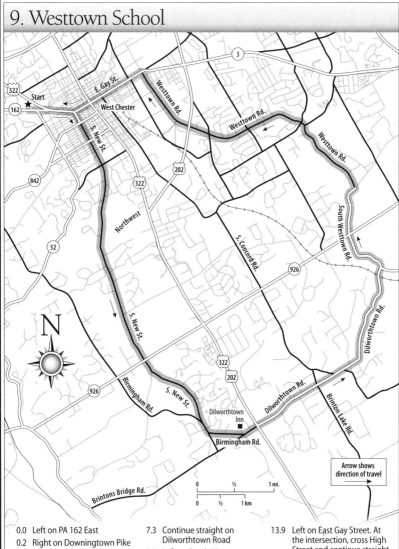

Arrow shows
direction of travel

0   ½   1 mi.

0   ½   1 km

0.0	Left on PA 162 East	
0.2	Right on Downingtown Pike	
0.5	Bear right on S. New Street and follow it through town	
3.9	Cross PA 926; continue on South New Street	
5.0	Left on Birmingham Road	
5.8	Jog left onto Brintons Bridge Road, which becomes Dilworthtown Road after it crosses US 202	

7.3	Continue straight on Dilworthtown Road
8.7	Left on South Westtown Road
9.5	Cross PA 926 and continue on Westtown Road
10.2	Bear left at the Westtown School Gate
11.2	Bear left at the intersection to stay on Westtown Road

13.9	Left on East Gay Street. At the intersection, cross High Street and continue straight on Gay Street
15.4	Right on North Bradford Street
15.6	Left at the light and then right into the lot
15.7	Return to start

9

Westtown School

- **DISTANCE:** 15.7 miles
- **TERRAIN/DIFFICULTY:** City streets initially, then suburbs, then open country and rolling hills; moderate
- **START:** Parking lot of Bradford Plaza shopping center in West Chester
- **GPS COORDINATES OF START:** N39 57.601' / W75 37.242'
- **GETTING THERE/PARKING:** From US 202/322, take the PA 3 exit and drive straight through West Chester until you reach the intersection of PA 162 and PA 322. Bradford Plaza is just beyond this intersection on the right side on PA 162.
- **HIGHLIGHTS:** West Chester University, Westtown School

This ride begins on the west side of this university town and county seat, crosses the center of the city—giving you a chance to see the Greek Revival architecture for which it is renowned—and emerges into the rural countryside. At a little more than 5 miles you will pass the Dilworthtown Inn, just as Washington's army did after its defeat in the Battle of the Brandywine in 1777.

The turnaround point is the gate of Westtown School, a private Quaker institution founded in 1799 on the same 600 acres it occupies today. This is the easternmost point of any of the rides in this book. The school owns and displays one of artist N. C. Wyeth's most popular paintings, *The Giant,* which shows a group of children at play on a beach while they gaze in wonderment at a club-wielding giant who materializes from clouds over the ocean. While Westtown School undergoes renovations, it has lent the painting to the Brandywine River Museum.

On this ride you'll pass the Dilworthtown Inn, just as George Washington did in 1777.

The Wyeth family of artists has a long and rich association with Chester County. The home and studio of N. C. Wyeth, illustrator and family patriarch, has been designated a National Historical Landmark; tours are available through the Brandywine River Museum in nearby Chadds Ford. Four of his five children are accomplished artists, the most famous of whom is the late Andrew. His son Nathaniel was an engineer for DuPont and held the patent for the recyclable plastic soda bottle. His grandson Jamie is a famous painter, and another grandson, Howard, a musician, gained fame as a drummer for Bob Dylan. Numerous works of these artists as well as lesser-known family members are on display in the Brandywine River Museum.

0.0 Turn left on PA 162 East.

0.2 Turn right on Downingtown Pike.

0.5 Bear right on South New Street and follow it all the way through town.

3.9 Cross PA 926; continue on South New Street.

5.0 Turn left on Birmingham Road.

5.8 Jog left onto Brintons Bridge Road, which becomes Dilworthtown Road after it crosses US 202.

7.3 Continue straight on Dilworthtown Road.

8.7 Turn left on South Westtown Road.

9.5 Cross PA 926 and continue on Westtown Road.

10.2 Bear left at the Westtown School Gate.

11.2 Bear left at the intersection to stay on Westtown Road.

13.9 Turn left on East Gay Street and continue through the center of the old town. At the intersection, cross High Street and continue straight on Gay Street.

15.4 Turn right on North Bradford Street.

15.6 Turn left at the light and then right into the Bradford Plaza lot.

15.7 Return to start.

SOUTHERN
CHESTER COUNTY

Minguannan Indian Town marker

THE SOUTHERNMOST CORNER of Chester County is bordered by Octoraro Creek, which separates it from Lancaster County to the west, the Maryland border to the south, the Delaware border to the east, and US 1 to the north. The northern border is arbitrary, and ride 13 actually crosses it.

Each of these four rides starts in one of the small communities that originated as commercial centers for the surrounding farms and mines. The countryside is occupied mostly by farms, some of which are Amish. Ride 13 passes Lincoln University, a historic African American school, while ride 11 passes through beautiful southern Chester County countryside. Ride 12 passes close to some serpentine barrens, crosses into Maryland, and returns to Chester County across an exquisite little covered bridge. Ride 10 spends miles in the beautiful White Clay Creek Preserve in Pennsylvania and Delaware, and passes the Arc Corner monument.

Tourism Information

There are some restaurants and shops for provisions in the towns, but no hotels.

www.cometooxford.com

www.cometowestgrove.com

Bicycle Shops

I know of no bike shops in this immediate area. The closest would be in Newark, Delaware, or the Wilmington area.

10. Arc Corner

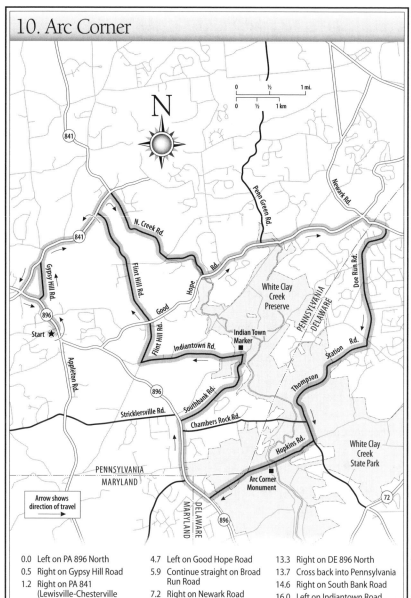

0.0	Left on PA 896 North	
0.5	Right on Gypsy Hill Road	
1.2	Right on PA 841 (Lewisville-Chesterville Road)	
2.7	Right on North Creek Road	
3.9	Enter White Clay Creek Preserve. Cross bridge and turn left on North Creek Road	
4.7	Left on Good Hope Road	
5.9	Continue straight on Broad Run Road	
7.2	Right on Newark Road	
7.7	Right on Doe Run Road	
9.5	Continue straight through this intersection	
11.6	Right on Hopkins Road	
13.3	Right on DE 896 North	
13.7	Cross back into Pennsylvania	
14.6	Right on South Bank Road	
16.0	Left on Indiantown Road	
17.5	Right on Flint Hill Road	
19.9	Left on PA 841	
21.6	Left on PA 896	
22.5	Right into school parking lot	

10

Arc Corner

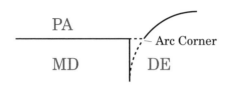

- **DISTANCE:** 22.5 miles

- **TERRAIN/DIFFICULTY:** Mostly woodlands and rolling hills, extended segment along White Clay Creek; moderate because of some hills

- **START:** Parking lot of Avon Grove Charter School in Kemblesville, Pennsylvania

- **GPS COORDINATES OF START:** N39 45.062' / W75 49.535'

- **GETTING THERE/PARKING:** The ride begins in the school parking lot, which is on the right side of PA 896, 0.5 mile south of Kemblesville Methodist Cemetery

- **HIGHLIGHTS:** White Clay Creek Preserve, Arc Corner, Indian town, meetinghouse

In 1750 the Delaware-Pennsylvania boundary was defined by an arc extending 12 miles from the cupola of the courthouse in New Castle, Delaware. This has often been called the Twelve-Mile Circle. It extends eastward to the low-tide mark on the New Jersey shore of the Delaware River, then southward until a more conventional boundary is established in the middle of the channel of the Delaware River estuary. There is an ongoing boundary dispute to this day between these two states involving construction of an energy facility. To the west the arc cuts past the northeastern edge of Maryland; this anomaly was corrected by the Mason-Dixon survey (see ride 2).

Even the Mason-Dixon survey failed to correct one additional boundary dispute, which provides a point of interest on this ride. On the small figure at the beginning of this ride (above), you can see the tiny wedge of territory claimed by both Pennsylvania and Delaware,

Quaker meetinghouse and cemetery, South Bank Road

an area about 0.75 mile along its top edge and about 3 miles south-westward along the arc. The Arc Corner is located at GPS coordinates N39 43.324' / W75 46.413' and is marked by a small stone monument you can visit on this ride. This dispute was finally resolved in 1921 when it was mutually agreed that "the wedge" belonged to Delaware because it lies south of the east–west Mason-Dixon Line.

During the more than 150 years of this territorial uncertainty, "the wedge" had a reputation for lawlessness because neither Pennsylvania nor Delaware saw fit to have an adequate law-enforcement presence in someone else's territory. The same was reputedly true of some areas along the Delaware River shore of New Jersey, which fell within the Delaware Twelve-Mile Circle.

You will see another point of historical interest at a tranquil back-roads intersection on the return loop of this ride. Where South Bank Road meets London Tract/Indiantown Road there is a stone marker, which commemorates the sale of Delaware Indian land (between the Delaware River and the Chesapeake Bay to the falls of the Susquehanna River) by Chief Owhala of the Unami group to William Penn in 1683.

A substantial part of this ride takes you through the White Clay Creek Preserve of Pennsylvania and White Clay Creek State Park in Delaware, both wonderfully cool, lush tracts of riverine forest. It starts in some high, open country outside of the little town of Kemblesville, Pennsylvania, then swings north and east to cross into Delaware on Newark Road. After turning south on Doe Run Road and passing through the tiny settlement of Corner Ketch, you enter the White Clay Creek Preserve on Thompson Station Road, which takes you along the creek to Hopkins Bridge Road. After you turn right on this road, watch for the Arc Corner monument about a mile farther on the left. Continue on this road and return to DE 896. A right turn brings you back into Pennsylvania.

A right turn on South Bank Road brings you back into the White Clay and the Quaker meetinghouse at the site of Minguannan Indian Town. This is a beautiful spot and worth a pause. From here you will climb back up out of the creek valley and work your way back to the start.

0.0 Turn left on PA 896 North.

0.5 Turn right on Gypsy Hill Road.

1.2 Turn right on PA 841 (Lewisville-Chesterville Road).

2.7 Turn right on North Creek Road.

3.9 Enter White Clay Creek Preserve. Cross the bridge and turn left on North Creek Road.

4.7 Turn left on Good Hope Road.

5.9 Continue straight on Broad Run Road.

7.2 Turn right on Newark Road.
On this stretch you cross into Delaware, where the road name changes to Little Baltimore Road.

7.7 Turn right on Doe Run Road. Continue on this road straight into White Clay Creek Preserve and stay next to the creek.
This is a beautiful, shady, narrow road through the preserve. Ignore the signs that say it is closed; bicyclists will be able to continue. On some maps it is called Thompson Station Road.

9.5 Continue straight through this intersection.

11.6 Turn right on Hopkins Road.

This is in the Arc Circle. Some maps call this Hopkins Bridge Road. About 1 mile on the left, look for the stone monument, called the Arc Obelisk, marking the Arc Corner.

13.3 Turn right on DE 896 North.

13.7 Cross back into Pennsylvania.

14.6 Turn right on South Bank Road.

16.0 Turn left on Indiantown Road and ride uphill out of the creek valley.

This is the site of Minguannan Indian Town of the Unami group of the Lenni-Lenape, or Delaware, tribe. There is a cemetery, meetinghouse, and a commemorative stone monument at this intersection.

17.5 Turn right on Flint Hill Road.

19.9 Turn left on PA 841.

21.6 Turn left on PA 896.

22.5 Turn right into the school parking lot.

11

West Grove

- **DISTANCE:** 19.8 miles
- **TERRAIN/DIFFICULTY:** Gentle, rolling hills; easy
- **START:** Rear parking lot of Jennersville Regional Hospital
- **GPS COORDINATES OF START:** N39 49.267' / W75 53.335'
- **GETTING THERE/PARKING:** From US 1, take the PA 796 exit south, and in 0.1 mile turn right on West Baltimore Pike. The hospital is 0.8 mile from this intersection on the left. Enter the last driveway and drive to the large lot behind the buildings.
- **HIGHLIGHTS:** Woodlands and open country

This ride takes you through some pleasant southern Chester County countryside. Almost 7 miles into this ride you will make a left turn onto London Grove Road; just before that there is a right turn for Spencer Road. Less than a quarter mile down Spencer Road is the Stroud Water Research Center, dedicated to the study of streams and rivers.

Affiliated with the University of Pennsylvania and the Academy of Natural Sciences in Philadelphia, the Stroud Center was founded in 1966 by the late Dick and Joan Stroud, on whose property the center sits, and Dr. Ruth Patrick, an eminent freshwater biologist. Dr. Patrick had done pioneering work on the water quality of Lancaster County's Conestoga Creek, and with the support of the Strouds she began to focus on the White Clay Creek watershed. That creek, which you encounter intimately on ride 10, literally runs through the Stroud Center, then through Chester County and into New Castle County, Delaware, where it flows into the Christina River and on into the

11. West Grove

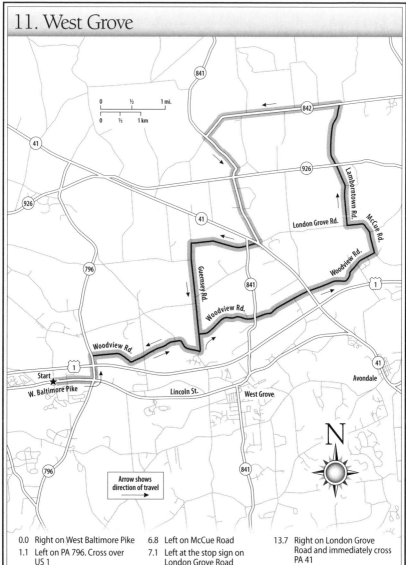

0.0 Right on West Baltimore Pike
1.1 Left on PA 796. Cross over US 1
1.5 Right on Woodview Road
2.1 Left at stop sign to continue on Woodview Road
3.4 Left on Guernsey Road
3.6 Right on Woodview Road
5.6 Cross PA 41

6.8 Left on McCue Road
7.1 Left at the stop sign on London Grove Road
7.6 Right on Lamborntown Road
8.5 Cross PA 926 (Street Road)
9.5 Left on Clonmell-Upland Road (PA 842)
11.8 Left on PA 841
12.6 Cross PA 926

13.7 Right on London Grove Road and immediately cross PA 41
14.8 Left on North Guernsey Road
16.4 Right on Woodview Road
18.3 Left on PA 796
18.7 Right on West Baltimore Pike
19.8 Left into hospital parking lot

Paul Woodward, © The Countryman Press

Horse pasture northeast of West Grove

Delaware River. Because of the Stroud Center's research efforts, the watershed has become one of the most studied headwaters in the world. The center, a research facility, is not open to the public.

The fruits of this research are not only of academic interest but are shared with preservation and conservancy groups that want to optimize their landscape and ecosystem preservation and restoration efforts. This is another opportunity for you to tip your helmet to some far-thinking individuals who have made possible the countryside through which you have been passing.

This ride is a loop that takes you north of US 1 into the countryside, east across PA 41, and back to West Grove from the northeast.

0.0 Turn right on West Baltimore Pike.

1.1 Turn left on PA 796. Cross over US 1.

1.5 Turn right on Woodview Road.

2.1 Turn left at the stop sign to continue on Woodview Road.

3.4 Turn left on Guernsey Road.

3.6 Turn right on Woodview Road.

5.6 Cross PA 41.

6.8 Turn left on McCue Road.

7.1 Turn left at the stop sign on London Grove Road.

7.6 Turn right on Lamborntown Road.

8.5 Cross PA 926 (Street Road).

9.5 Turn left on Clonmell-Upland Road (PA 842).

11.8 Turn left on PA 841.

12.6 Cross PA 926.

13.7 Turn right on London Grove Road and immediately cross PA 41, at the traffic light.

14.8 Turn left on North Guernsey Road.

16.4 Turn right on Woodview Road.

18.3 Turn left on PA 796.

18.7 Turn right on West Baltimore Pike.

19.8 Turn left into the hospital parking lot.

Nottingham

- **DISTANCE:** 22.8 miles
- **TERRAIN/DIFFICULTY:** Rolling hills; easy
- **START:** Parking lot of Oxford Area High School
- **GPS COORDINATES OF START:** N39 46.208' / W75 57.530'
- **GETTING THERE/PARKING:** The center of Oxford is the intersection of PA 10 and PA 472. Drive south on PA 472 for about 0.5 mile and turn right on Fifth Street. In about 1.5 miles turn left on Waterway Road. The high school is on the north side of the road in about 0.2 mile. Parking may be a problem during school hours.
- **HIGHLIGHTS:** Ride into Maryland, covered bridge, Amish farms

The ride explores the southwesternmost section of Chester County and crosses the Mason-Dixon Line into Maryland. At first it is suburban in character, then changes to rural as you ride south. There are some Amish farms, though not nearly as many as in Lancaster County.

After you cross back into Pennsylvania from Maryland on Little Elk Creek Road, you will cross the stream of the same name over the Glen Hope Covered Bridge. This is a very nice, shady crossing and worth a stop.

Later in the ride you will travel briefly on Chrome Road, which went to the once-thriving mining town of Chrome, today just a crossroads. This brings to mind one of the signal geologic features of this area, which is easy to miss. Northwestern Maryland and southeastern Pennsylvania have outcroppings of rock—called serpentine barrens—that are rich in certain minerals and metals. The barrens were not suitable for agriculture, so colonial settlers left them alone. The Lenni-

12. Nottingham

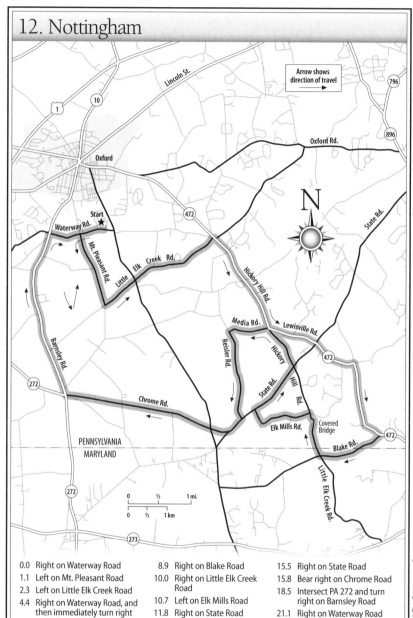

Arrow shows direction of travel

0.0 Right on Waterway Road	8.9 Right on Blake Road	15.5 Right on State Road
1.1 Left on Mt. Pleasant Road	10.0 Right on Little Elk Creek Road	15.8 Bear right on Chrome Road
2.3 Left on Little Elk Creek Road	10.7 Left on Elk Mills Road	18.5 Intersect PA 272 and turn right on Barnsley Road
4.4 Right on Waterway Road, and then immediately turn right on Hickory Hill Road (PA 472). Continue on PA 472	11.8 Right on State Road	21.1 Right on Waterway Road
	12.7 Left on Hickory Hill Road	22.8 Arrive back at start
	13.4 Left on Media Road	
6.0 Bear left to continue on PA 472	14.1 Left on Reisler Road	

Paul Woodward, © The Countryman Press

Glen Hope Covered Bridge

Lenape, however, had used the barrens as sources of soapstone, which they carved. In the early 1800s chrome was found in these barrens, and mining began; at one point this area had cornered the world market in that material, and the boomtown of Chrome was established. Although primarily used as a metal today, chrome was used at that time mostly in paints and tanning salts. Mining continued in the Nottingham barrens from the mid-1800s until the 1930s.

Chester County created the Nottingham County Park on the site of old mine works, and flooded pits and remnants of that industry can be found in the park, which is located just off US 1 southwest of Oxford. In the early 1990s the Nature Conservancy purchased the Chrome Serpentine Barrens in Elk Township, Maryland, to preserve endangered wildflowers that are only found there.

The ride circles back northward from Maryland to the start.

0.0 Turn right on Waterway Road.

1.1 Turn left on Mt. Pleasant Road.

2.3 Turn left on Little Elk Creek Road.

4.4 Turn right on Waterway Road, and then immediately turn right on Hickory Hill Road (PA 472). Continue on PA 472.

6.0 Bear left to continue on PA 472.

8.9 Turn right on Blake Road.
You're now in the state of Maryland.

10.0 Turn right on Little Elk Creek Road.
There is a covered bridge at 10.4 miles that is worth a stop. The road name changes to Hickory Hill Road at this point.

10.7 Turn left on Elk Mills Road.
At 11.4 miles the road name changes to Rogers Road.

11.8 Turn right on State Road.

12.7 Turn left on Hickory Hill Road.

13.4 Turn left on Media Road.

14.1 Turn left on Reisler Road.

15.5 Turn right on State Road.

15.8 Bear right on Chrome Road.

18.5 Intersect PA 272 and turn right on Barnsley Road.

21.1 Turn right on Waterway Road.

22.8 Arrive back at the high school parking lot.

Oxford—Lincoln University

- **DISTANCE:** 19 miles
- **TERRAIN/DIFFICULTY:** Rolling hills; easy
- **START:** Oxford Cemetery
- **GPS COORDINATES OF START:** N39 47.443' / W75 58.905'
- **GETTING THERE/PARKING:** The center of Oxford is the intersection of PA 10 and PA 472. The Oxford Cemetery Association is 0.4 mile north on the right side of Pine Street, which becomes Scroggy Road. Please be sure to park on the pavement and not on the grass.
- **HIGHLIGHTS:** Farmland, historic African American university

After you leave the northern suburbs of Oxford, you ride into the country to enjoy the rural landscape. It is worth contemplating that this landscape has dramatically changed over the past millennium. Prior to the arrival of white settlers, this area was part of an immense forest that stretched almost unbroken as far as the Mississippi Valley. Except for some small cleared areas used by Native Americans as croplands and the stunted growth overlying the serpentine barrens (see ride 12), this area was a primeval forest of hardwood trees of such enormous size that it is difficult for us to imagine them today.

Before fossil fuels became available, there were two sources of power in this area besides human and animal muscle: the burning of wood from the forests and the flow of water in the rivers and streams. This changed the landscape forever. The first-growth forests were all logged for timber, firewood, fences, and charcoal, yielding a ruined landscape of eroded soil, much of which was planted with crops. Along nearly every significant watercourse were mill races and ponds direct-

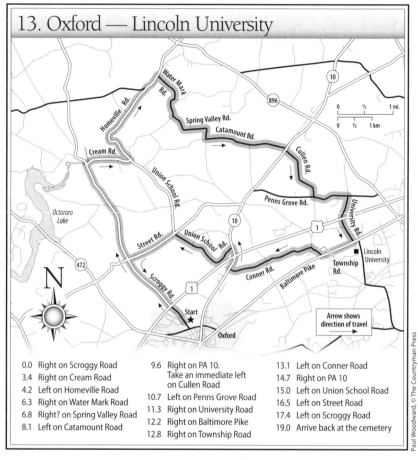

13. Oxford — Lincoln University

0.0	Right on Scroggy Road	9.6	Right on PA 10. Take an immediate left on Cullen Road	13.1	Left on Conner Road
3.4	Right on Cream Road			14.7	Right on PA 10
4.2	Left on Homeville Road			15.0	Left on Union School Road
6.3	Right on Water Mark Road	10.7	Left on Penns Grove Road	16.5	Left on Street Road
6.8	Right? on Spring Valley Road	11.3	Right on University Road	17.4	Left on Scroggy Road
8.1	Left on Catamount Road	12.2	Right on Baltimore Pike	19.0	Arrive back at the cemetery
		12.8	Right on Township Road		

Paul Woodward, © The Countryman Press

ing the flow of the streams to the mills, which stood almost elbow to elbow along the banks. There were many hundreds of mills in Chester and Lancaster counties, only a few of which can be seen today. Their presence is reflected in local town and road names. Many of these mills were flour mills, while others were for sawing timber, or stamping iron from nearby iron mines and furnaces. Their operations ruined the counties' watercourses for generations, and what you see today is the result of restoration by both nature and man.

None of the woodlands you see on any of these rides are virgin forest, however. At most, the trees are 60 to 100 years old, with some isolated older specimens. Much forest was regenerated from fields that were allowed to lie fallow, while some trees were deliberately replanted as windbreaks, for timber, or as the result of conservation efforts.

Some of the mills have been preserved or restored as historical sites, but the most interesting, in my opinion, is Rohrer's Mill, located east of Strasburg in Lancaster County, which still operates commercially as a flour mill. It is open for visitors, and the owner will gladly engage the venerable mechanisms for you so that you can experience the sounds and motion of the old building, which seems almost like a living thing. Oh, you can also buy a sack of flour milled by the old stones. My wife says it's particularly good for baking.

At 12.2 miles you will pass the campus of Lincoln University of the Commonwealth of Pennsylvania, a historic African American institution that counts among its alumni the poet Langston Hughes and Justice Thurgood Marshall. Chartered before the Civil War and the Emancipation Proclamation in 1854 as the Ashmun Institute, it was renamed after President Lincoln in 1866. One of its early presidents described it as "the first institution found anywhere in the world to provide a higher education in the arts and sciences for male youth of

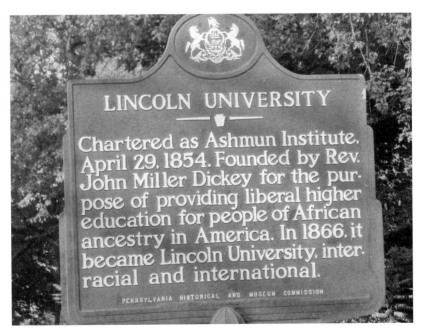

Lincoln University historical marker

African descent." Today it is coeducational and boasts an interracial and international student body of about two thousand. According to its Web site, it graduated in its first one hundred years more than 20 percent of all Black American physicians and more than 10 percent of all Black American lawyers.

0.0 Turn right on Scroggy Road.

3.4 Turn right on Cream Road.

4.2 Turn left on Homeville Road.

6.3 Turn right on Water Mark Road.

6.8 Turn right on Spring Valley Road.
There is some confusion of road signs between Muddy Run Road and Spring Valley Road. Just stay on the main thoroughfare.

8.1 Turn left on Catamount Road.

9.6 Turn right on PA 10. Take an immediate left on Cullen Road.

10.7 Turn left on Penns Grove Road.

11.3 Turn right on University Road.

12.2 Turn right on Baltimore Pike.
Lincoln University is located at this intersection.

12.8 Turn right on Township Road.

13.1 Turn left on Conner Road.

14.7 Turn right on PA 10.

15.0 Turn left on Union School Road.

16.5 Turn left on Street Road.

17.4 Turn left on Scroggy Road.

19.0 Arrive back at the cemetery.

WESTERN
CHESTER COUNTY

Mercer's Mill Covered Bridge

AS IN NEARBY WEST MARLBOROUGH TOWNSHIP, much of the land in West Fallowfield Township is devoted to horse breeding. The country-side is a little less open here than it is in the east, and the hills are a little more sharply undulating. As you approach Octoraro Creek, the forested areas become denser, and the lush greenery of the stream valley takes over. Although Hibernia County Park is close to Coatesville, you will remain in the surrounding countryside and avoid the congestion and traffic of that city. Octoraro Creek no longer forms the county border this far north, and the transition into Amish Country is even more dramatic without it.

These three rides allow you to explore some of the area where Chester County borders eastern Lancaster County. Rides 14 and 15 keep you west of busy PA 41 and approach Octoraro Creek, which forms the county border at this point. Ride 15 crosses the creek on a splendid covered bridge and stays close to it for 4 miles on a narrow, shaded road. Ride 14 parallels PA 41, then turns west toward the creek. After it turns north along Knights Run, it swings back to PA 41. Ride 16 starts in Hibernia County Park, north of Coatesville, and takes you directly into Lancaster County to the west, where you will begin to see Amish farms. The ride then loops back to the park, which is worth exploring.

Tourism Information

There are motels and restaurants along US 30 and in Downingtown and West Chester.

www.americantowns.com/pa/coatesville

http://dsf.chesco.org/ccparks (Hibernia Park)

www.pabred.com (Pennsylvania Horse Breeders Association)

www.vet.upenn.edu (New Bolton Center)

Bicycle Shops

The Downingtown Bicycle Shop, 833 West Lancaster Avenue, Downingtown; 610-269-5626

Shirk's Bike Shop, 1649 Ligalaw Road, East Earl; 717-445-5731

14

Cochranville

- **DISTANCE:** 17 miles
- **TERRAIN/DIFFICULTY:** Rolling hills; easy
- **START:** U.S. Post Office parking lot on PA 41 in Cochranville
- **GPS COORDINATES OF START:** N39 53.638' / W75 55.295'
- **GETTING THERE/PARKING:** The post office is 0.1 mile north of the intersection of PA 10 and PA 41 on the west side of PA 41. If this lot is filled, there are other business parking lots nearby, and there is a cemetery immediately north of the post office.
- **HIGHLIGHTS:** Horse farms, open countryside

Once you get away from PA 41 on this ride, what you will mostly see are a lot of horse breeding farms. This is big business in Pennsylvania; combined with horse racing, it contributes about $600 million to the Commonwealth's economy. The headquarters of the Pennsylvania Horse Breeders Association is in Kennett Square in Chester County, and its mission is to encourage the breeding of Thoroughbreds in Pennsylvania. Race horses and polo ponies are either Thoroughbreds or Thoroughbred crosses.

If you like to see horses, you will see plenty of them on the rides in this section. Behind the board fences in Chester County you are most likely to see Thoroughbreds and polo ponies, with a few breeds like Friesians for carriage teams. Some farms specialize in less-common breeds like Welsh ponies. The same is true of Lancaster County, with more emphasis on some rarer breeds. In the Amish farming areas you will see huge draft horses and mules that the Amish breed as draft animals. The Amish use standardbreds or standard crosses to pull their carriages and much larger draft horses like Percherons for their

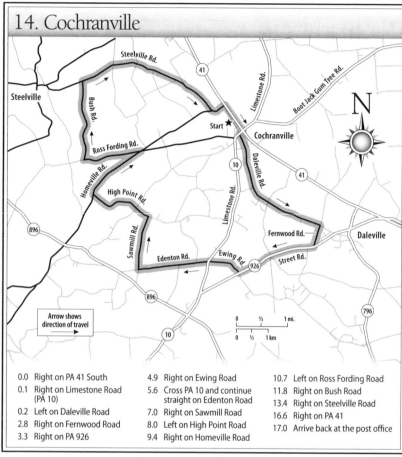

14. Cochranville

0.0 Right on PA 41 South	4.9 Right on Ewing Road	10.7 Left on Ross Fording Road
0.1 Right on Limestone Road (PA 10)	5.6 Cross PA 10 and continue straight on Edenton Road	11.8 Right on Bush Road
0.2 Left on Daleville Road	7.0 Right on Sawmill Road	13.4 Right on Steelville Road
2.8 Right on Fernwood Road	8.0 Left on High Point Road	16.6 Right on PA 41
3.3 Right on PA 926	9.4 Right on Homeville Road	17.0 Arrive back at the post office

Paul Woodward. © The Countryman Press

larger wagons. The horses that draw the carriages in New York City's Central Park are purchased from Lancaster County Amish farmers.

If you are really interested in horses, the New Bolton Center of the University of Pennsylvania School of Veterinary Medicine is located on PA 926 about 10 miles southeast of Cochranville. This is where Barbaro was treated after his ultimately mortal injuries at the Preakness in 2007.

0.0 Turn right on PA 41 South.

0.1 Turn right on Limestone Road.
This is also named PA 10.

0.2 Turn left on Daleville Road.

2.8 Turn right on Fernwood Road.

3.3 Turn right on PA 926 (Street Road).

4.9 Turn right on Ewing Road.

5.6 Cross PA 10 and continue straight on Edenton Road.

7.0 Turn right on Sawmill Road.

8.0 Turn left on High Point Road.

9.4 Turn right on Homeville Road.

10.7 Turn left on Ross Fording Road.

11.8 Turn right on Bush Road.
The road surface changes from pavement to packed gravel at 12 miles and changes back to pavement at 12.6 miles. The road is level.

13.4 Turn right on Steelville Road.

16.6 Turn right on PA 41.

17.0 Arrive back at the post office.

A mare and her foal west of Cochranville

15

Atglen—Bailey Bridge

DISTANCE: 21.3 miles

TERRAIN/DIFFICULTY: Rolling hills, mostly flat; easy

START: Parking lot of Penningtonville Presbyterian Church on Main Street in Atglen

GPS COORDINATES OF START: N39 56.816' / W75 58.358'

GETTING THERE/PARKING: From PA 41, take PA 372 west about 0.2 mile to Main Street. The church parking lot is on the southwest corner of the intersection. Please do not use this lot during Sunday services.

HIGHLIGHTS: Old town of Atglen, East Branch of Octoraro Creek, covered bridge

This ride is really about Octoraro Creek, which forms the Lancaster–Chester County border at this point. As you approach the covered Bailey Bridge, take a few minutes to stop and savor this wonderful place. Lean your bike against the fence or bridge abutment and see the purple-stemmed cliffbrake ferns growing in the stone crevices. This is not a common fern, but it seems to like it here. Step down over the short wall on the left and walk beneath the bridge. This affords a cool, shady view of this languid little stream, with the bridge timbers and trees reflected on the water's surface, and leaves floating by. If you are wearing polarized sunglasses, you may see a few trout facing the current in the shade.

After you cross this small bridge and turn left, you will follow the creek for about 4 miles, after which the road ascends out of the stream valley onto some higher ground. This gradual climb sets the stage for a

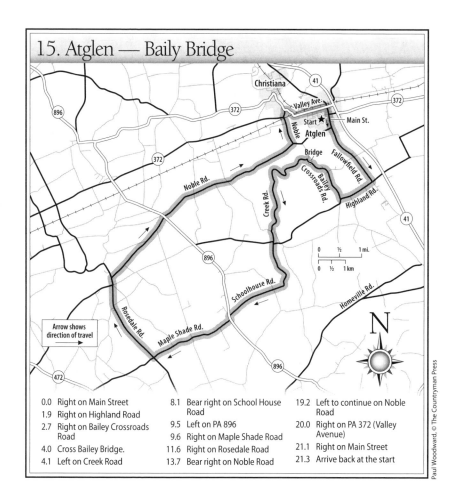

15. Atglen — Baily Bridge

0.0	Right on Main Street	
1.9	Right on Highland Road	
2.7	Right on Bailey Crossroads Road	
4.0	Cross Bailey Bridge.	
4.1	Left on Creek Road	
8.1	Bear right on School House Road	
9.5	Left on PA 896	
9.6	Right on Maple Shade Road	
11.6	Right on Rosedale Road	
13.7	Bear right on Noble Road	
19.2	Left to continue on Noble Road	
20.0	Right on PA 372 (Valley Avenue)	
21.1	Right on Main Street	
21.3	Arrive back at the start	

Paul Woodward, © The Countryman Press

nice 6.4-mile downhill ride back into Atglen.

Pennsylvania has more than two hundred covered bridges, more than any other state, and most of them are in Lancaster and Chester counties. Bailey Bridge, more properly called Mercer's Mill Covered Bridge, has the official designation of East Octoraro #2 Bridge. It is constructed of oak planks and is of a Burr arch truss design with steel hanger rods. Like all Lancaster County covered bridges, it is painted red inside and out, with white approaches.

There is much speculation about why covered bridges are covered. The most rational explanation from an engineering perspective is that a wooden span left exposed to the elements has a life span of about

A young bicyclist takes a rest at Mercer's Mill Covered Bridge.

nine years, while a covered span can last 80 or more years. Another less-compelling explanation is that when livestock are led through a covered bridge, they are less likely to panic because the bridge looks like a barn, a place in which they are comfortable, rather than a precarious and threatening passageway over a torrent.

0.0 Turn right on Main Street.

This is also named Fallowfield Road and Old Gap Newport Pike.

1.9 Turn right on Highland Road.

2.7 Turn right on Bailey Crossroads Road.

4.0 Cross Bailey Bridge.

4.1 Turn left on Creek Road.

8.1 Bear right on School House Road.

9.5 Turn left on PA 896.

9.6 Turn right on Maple Shade Road.

11.6 Turn right on Rosedale Road.

At 13.5 miles, after it crosses Bartville Road, Rosedale Road becomes Noble Road.

13.7 Bear right on Noble Road.

This begins a long downhill coast.

19.2 Turn left to continue on Noble Road.

20.0 Turn right on PA 372 (Valley Avenue).

21.1 Turn right on Main Street.

21.3 Arrive back at the start.

16. Hibernia Park

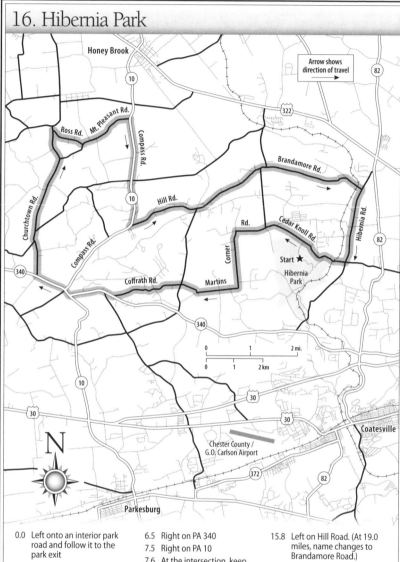

Honey Brook

Arrow shows direction of travel →

Ross Rd.　Mt. Pleasant Rd.

Compass Rd.

Churchtown Rd.

Compass Rd.

Hill Rd.

Brandamore Rd.

Cedar Knoll Rd.

Hibernia Rd.

Rd.

Corner

Start ★

Hibernia Park

Coffrath Rd.

Martins

Coatesville

Chester County / G.O. Carlson Airport

Parkesburg

N

0.0　Left onto an interior park road and follow it to the park exit

0.8　Left on Cedar Knoll Road

1.8　Jog slightly left on Martins Corner Road

2.4　Left to stay on Martins Corner Road (signs say Brandywine Drive)

4.5　Jog right, then straight on Coffrath Road

6.5　Right on PA 340

7.5　Right on PA 10

7.6　At the intersection, keep riding straight on PA 340

8.9　Right on Churchtown Road

11.6　Turn sharply right and back on Ross Road

12.3　Left on Mt. Pleasant Road

13.5　Right on PA 10 (Compass Road)

15.8　Left on Hill Road. (At 19.0 miles, name changes to Brandamore Road.)

21.4　Right on Hibernia Road

22.9　Right on Cedar Knoll Road

23.5　Left to enter the park

23.9　Return to parking lot

Paul Woodward, © The Countryman Press

16

Hibernia Park

- **DISTANCE:** 23.9 miles
- **TERRAIN/DIFFICULTY:** Rolling hills; easy
- **START:** Parking lot in Hibernia Park
- **GPS COORDINATES OF START:** N40 01.800' / W75 50.499'
- **GETTING THERE/PARKING:** From US 30, take PA 82 North for about 2 miles and turn left on Cedar Knoll Road. Follow the signs to the park entrance, which is on the left. Park in the lot near the mansion.
- **HIGHLIGHTS:** Historic park, Lancaster County, migratory birds at nearby Marsh Creek State Park

The starting point of this ride is Hibernia County Park near Coatesville. The park comprises 900 acres of trees, fields, hiking trails, a 90-acre lake, and a mile of the West Branch of the Brandywine River. Hibernia Mansion, on the grounds, was once the home of the ironmasters who ran the iron furnace and mills that occupied the site for almost two centuries. Around 1900 the mansion became the country estate of a prosperous Philadelphia lawyer. After it had been abandoned for 15 years, the property was purchased by Chester County Parks and Recreation and refurbished.

After leaving the park, you will soon cross into Lancaster County and begin to see Amish farms. Circling back, you will reenter Hibernia Park from the north. Less than 10 miles to the northeast is Marsh Creek State Park, which is renowned for sightings of migratory birds in season.

Amish farm, eastern Lancaster County

0.0 Turn left out of the lot onto an interior park road and follow it to the park exit.

0.8 Turn left on Cedar Knoll Road.

1.8 Jog slightly left on Martins Corner Road.

2.4 Turn left to stay on Martins Corner Road (signs say BRANDYWINE DRIVE). *Stay on this road; it turns quite a bit.*

4.5 Jog right, then straight on Coffrath Road.

6.5 Turn right on PA 340.

7.5 Turn right on PA 10.

7.6 At the intersection, keep riding straight on PA 340.

8.9 Turn right on Churchtown Road.

Notice the Amish schoolhouse on the right. You are now in Lancaster County.

11.6 Turn sharply right and back on Ross Road.

12.3 Turn left on Mt. Pleasant Road.

13.5 Turn right on PA 10 (Compass Road).

15.8 Turn left on Hill Road.

Stay on this road. When it crosses Birdell Road at 19.0 miles, its name changes to Brandamore Road.

21.4 Turn right on Hibernia Road.

22.9 Turn right on Cedar Knoll Road.

23.5 Turn left to enter the park.

23.9 Return to parking lot.

NORTHERN
CHESTER COUNTY

Giant sycamores like these are common along Chester County streams

I WANTED TO INCLUDE A RIDE from this corner of Chester County because it is not yet heavily developed and there are many great places for bicycling, especially around French Creek State Park, Marsh Creek Park, and Struble Lake. To the east and south, the density of development and traffic increase quite suddenly; to the north and west are the borders of Berks and Montgomery counties.

Ride 17 will give you a good sample of what this countryside is like and stays well off the beaten track. There is a nice little rural island here, and Nantmeal Village is near the center of it. A segment of this ride follows the Horseshoe Trail, which is described in the ride text.

Tourism Information

Nearby Exton has a number of chain hotels, as well as restaurants and services.

www.saintpetersvillage.com

www.greenvalleys.org

www.dcnr.state.pa.us/stateparks/parks/frenchcreek

Bicycle Shops

Bike Line of Exton, 292 East Lincoln Highway, Exton; 610-594-9380

Exton Bicycles, 337 East Lincoln Highway, Exton; 610-363-2747

17. Nantmeal Village — Horseshoe Trail

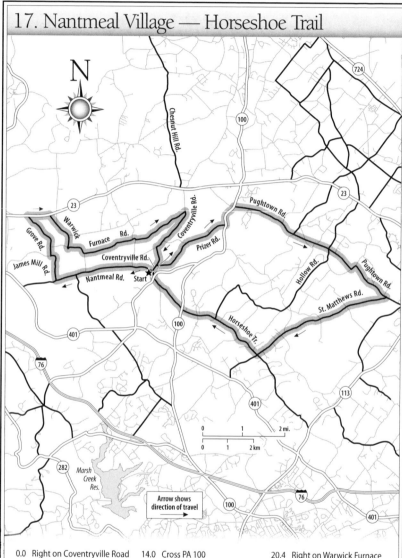

0.0	Right on Coventryville Road	
0.3	Right on Prizer Road	
2.5	Left on PA 100	
3.0	Right on Pughtown Road	
6.5	Jog left to stay on Pughtown Road	
7.8	Right on St. Matthews Road	
11.6	Right on Horseshoe Trail	
14.0	Cross PA 100	
15.1	Pass the starting point and continue up Coventryville Road	
15.2	Left on Nantmeal Road	
17.8	Right on James Mill Road	
18.6	Right on Grove Road	
19.9	Right on PA 23	
20.4	Right on Warwick Furnace Road	
23.4	Cross Iron Bridge and turn left to continue on Warwick Furnace Road	
24.8	Right on Coventryville Road	
26.0	Left to continue on Coventryville Road	
26.8	Arrive back at parking area	

Paul Woodward, © The Countryman Press

Nantmeal Village— Horseshoe Trail

- **DISTANCE:** 26.8 miles
- **TERRAIN/DIFFICULTY:** Rolling hills; easy
- **START:** Roadside parking apron across Nantmeal Road from the United Methodist Church
- **GPS COORDINATES OF START:** N40 08.521' / W75 42.290'
- **GETTING THERE/PARKING:** About 4 miles north of US 76 (the Pennsylvania Turnpike) on PA 100 North, turn left on the Horseshoe Trail. Continue for 1.1 miles into Nantmeal Village. The church is prominently visible on the left, and the parking area is on the roadside directly opposite. Please do not park here during Sunday services.
- **HIGHLIGHTS:** Old village of Nantmeal, nearby St. Peters Village, open countryside

Nantmeal Village is a comfortable little place to begin this ride, which can be done in either direction. If you start by riding east on the Horseshoe Trail, you will have a pretty stiff mile-long uphill before you get warmed up. These directions assume you would prefer a gentler start. Nantmeal was settled by the Welsh in the 18th century, and the name means something like "sweet brook" in that language. The only thing remarkable about it is that it remains a peaceful rural oasis considering the urbanization and the industrial history of the surrounding area.

The Horseshoe Trail is a 140-mile-long hiking and equestrian trail running from Valley Forge to the Appalachian Trail just north of Hershey. It passes through five counties, and in the Chester County stretch about one-third of it travels on paved public roads, as does the segment on this ride. It is maintained by the Horseshoe Trail Club (P.O. Box 182, Birchrunville, PA 19421-0182), which can supply you with maps and information.

Near the beginning of the ride you will pass Welkinweir, an estate and arboretum administered by the Green Valleys Association (1368 Prizer Road, Pottstown, PA 19465; 610-469-7543). It is on the right side of Prizer Road about 1.5 miles from the start. It is open daily without charge to the public.

When you are riding along the ridges, you will see a large, solitary plume on the northeast horizon; this is the steam from the cooling towers of Limerick Nuclear Power Plant on the Schuylkill River.

There are two more attractions in the immediate vicinity: one is French Creek State Park a few miles to the northwest, and the other is the village of St. Peters, just north of Knauertown on PA 23. St. Peters is an old quarry and iron-making company town that has been transformed into an artists' colony. It's a nice place to relax and have lunch after your ride.

Basically, the first half of the ride is in high open countryside with great views, and the second is in a picturesque stream valley.

0.0 Turn right on Coventryville Road.

This road has two other names: Horseshoe Trail and Nantmeal Road. The sign in town says COVENTRYVILLE ROAD.

0.3 Turn right on Prizer Road.

2.5 Turn left on PA 100.

3.0 Turn right on Pughtown Road.

6.5 Jog left to stay on Pughtown Road.

7.8 Turn right on St. Matthews Road.

11.6 Turn right on Horseshoe Trail.

14.0 Cross PA 100.

15.1 Pass the starting point and continue up Coventryville Road.

Farm pond along Nantmeal Road

15.2 Turn left on Nantmeal Road.

17.8 Turn right on James Mill Road.

18.6 Turn right on Grove Road.

19.9 Turn right on PA 23.
This road has a good shoulder and smooth pavement.

20.4 Turn right on Warwick Furnace Road.

23.4 Cross Iron Bridge and turn left to continue on Warwick Furnace Road.

24.8 Turn right on Coventryville Road.

26.0 Turn left to continue on Coventryville Road.

26.8 Arrive back at the parking area.

Lancaster County

—

LANCASTER COUNTY BECAME Pennsylvania's fourth county in 1729 when it was split off from Chester County. The first European settlers arrived around 1710, attracted by the availability of water power and the deep, rich, fertile soil, which earned it the appellation Garden Spot of America. Before that the Susquehannocks, an Iroquois tribe, had dwelt here for millennia.

If you wish, you can visit the oldest standing European house in the county, the Hans Herr House, built in 1719 by one of the earliest Mennonite settlers. There is much of historical interest in this area, home of the famed Pennsylvania long rifle and the Conestoga wagon, but the main focus in terms of this guide is the back roads and countryside.

Half of the county's 984 square miles are zoned for agriculture, and there are more than five thousand farms, many of which are owned by Amish or Mennonite families. These farms provide the picturesque countryside through which we will ride. These are not just any farms, however; they are farms owned by the Plain People, so they give us a fascinating view into our past, available in few other rural areas. At first glance there may appear to be uniformity among these farm families, but there are actually about 25 separate groups of Amish, Mennonites, and Brethren in Lancaster County. For the sake of convenience, I'll refer to them collectively as Amish.

The Amish population in the United States approximately doubles every 20 years, and Amish families must sometimes travel to other parts of the country or Canada to purchase farmland for their children. There are concentrations of Amish in parts of Canada and the American Midwest, as well as in southern Delaware, Maryland, and other rural counties in Pennsylvania, but the largest is in Lancaster County. The average Amish farm is small relative to the average non-

Amish farm, with only about 50 acres under cultivation, all of which is worked with muscle power, both human and animal. Amish farms are labor-intensive operations employing the work of typically large families and an army of large draft horses and mules.

You will see Amish women and girls weeding their orderly vegetable and flower gardens by hand and mowing the lawns around their houses with hand mowers. The family washing will be hung out on long clotheslines to dry in the breeze. The men will be working the fields without tractors or combines, spreading manure for fertilizer, plowing behind teams of draft animals, and forking hay much like our non-Amish ancestors did more than two hundred years ago.

On Sunday you may see their carriages assembled on a farm where they are holding religious services. Amish don't have churches, but Mennonites do. Once I saw a wonderful Mennonite church: it was white and made of wood, surrounded by a high white picket fence and a canopy of large, green-leafed hardwood trees. In the parking lot were polished automobiles, every one of which was black.

On weekdays you may share the roads with Amish children riding bicycles, scooters, or roller skates to their one-roomed schoolhouses. Once I was on the side of a shady road taking a drink from my water bottle when I was startled by the sound of hooves on the pavement behind me. When I turned to look, four young Amish boys cantered past me, riding their ponies bareback. You will be riding through all of this while the Plain People conduct their lives, and you can see all of these things from a bicycle without intruding or gawking.

There are more than 200 covered bridges remaining in Pennsylvania from the more than 1,500 originally constructed. Lancaster County has 28 of them, more than any other county in the Commonwealth.

The rides in this section are deliberately designed to avoid major population centers and heavily trafficked roads, allowing you to experience the open, rural landscape in relative peace and safety. At some point you will stop for a rest or to enjoy the scenery, only to be nagged by the absence of something without quite realizing what that is. I'll tell you now: it's utility lines. Miles of Lancaster County roads don't have them because the Old Order Amish and Mennonites don't use electricity, telephones, or television due to their religious beliefs. Without the influence of the Amish, Lancaster County would have more utility lines, as well as fewer farms and more housing developments and shopping malls.

Most of these rides are in the southern parts of the county and along the Susquehanna River. The population density is higher and the land hillier in the northern and western parts of the county. The farther south and east you travel, the more the landscape opens into rolling hills and farmland. In the Susquehanna Valley, the woodlands are denser and the bluffs are higher along the east bank of the river, providing riding challenges and some spectacular scenery.

Interesting Reading

Hostetler, John A. *Amish Society.* 4th ed. Baltimore: Johns Hopkins University Press, 1993.

Tourism Information

www.lancastercountymuseums.org

www.lancasterheritage.com

www.padutchcountry.com

www.visitPA.com

Bicycle Shops

Green Mountain Cyclery, Inc., 285 South Reading Road, Ephrata; 717-859-2422

Martin's Bike Shop, 1194 Division Highway, Ephrata; 717-354-9157

Weaver's Bike Shop, 230 Sheaffer's School Road, Ephrata; 717-656-9385

Lancaster Bicycle Shop, 1138 Mannheim Pike, Lancaster; 717-299-9627

Full Circle Bicycle Shop, 145 East State Street, Quarryville; 717-786-9255

AMISH COUNTRY

THE FIVE RIDES IN THIS SECTION are all in the area east of Lancaster City, south of Ephrata, and west of Octoraro Creek. This is the heart of southeastern Pennsylvania's Amish farmland. Each ride will give you a good taste of this area, and if you take all of them, you will have seen most of what there is to see here. You will see many Amish farms, Mennonite churches, one-room Amish schoolhouses, tobacco barns, draft animals, and animal-powered farm machinery. You will also find yourself sharing the roads with these interesting people, and if you are discreet and friendly, you may even meet some.

Rides 18 and 19 both start in the parking lot of the Railroad Museum of Pennsylvania in Strasburg (as does ride 25 in the Susquehanna Valley section). This parking lot is conveniently located in the town of Strasburg, where you can find lodging, services (no bike shop), and many tourist attractions. If trains interest you, the railroad museum is excellent. Nearby is a toy train museum that has, among other things, an eye-popping display of brass engines. You can take a pleasant ride on the Strasburg Rail Road, visit the Amish Village, or take a ride through the countryside in an Amish buggy. About 2 miles east of town, a right turn off PA 741 onto Rohrer Mill Road will take you to an operating water-powered flour mill. While there, you can buy flour and baked goods.

Speaking of baked goods, one of the joys of visiting rural Lancaster County is the variety of homemade and homegrown foods you can buy at roadside farm stands, most of which are run by Amish farmers. (They are closed on Sunday.) There are many wood, leather, and metal items you can buy in this area, which are hard to find anywhere else, and Amish craftsmen are well and justly known for their skill and integrity. You just have to keep your eyes open for little hand-painted signs advertising HARNESS, FURNITURE, IRONMONGERY, BARRELS, and such things. Many Amish crafts businesses involve entire families.

Once I bought some cherry boards from an Amish woodworker, and, sensing a common interest, he showed me his impressively well-equipped shop of pneumatic tools powered by a kerosene-fueled compressor. He then asked me if I would like him to plane my boards and led me to another, smaller building in which he had a 3-foot-wide pneumatic planer. I still have a piece of masking tape I peeled off a back saw blade that says in pencil, "Not to mutch set." (The owner of the saw shop was communicating to his workers my preference that the teeth of the saw be narrowly set.) If you take the time, you can have many interesting experiences in Amish country.

Rides 20 and 21 take you through the northern part of this area, while ride 22 loops through the southern part, starting from the parking lot of the Robert Fulton House.

Tourism Information

www.strasburgpa.com

www.rrmuseumpa.org

www.padutch.com

www.iloveinns.com

Bicycle Shops

See the Lancaster County section.

18

Strasburg North

- **DISTANCE:** 17 miles
- **TERRAIN/DIFFICULTY:** Mostly flat; easy
- **START:** Parking lot just east of the Railroad Museum of Pennsylvania on PA 741 in Strasburg
- **GPS COORDINATES OF START:** N39 58.947' / W76 09.525'
- **GETTING THERE/PARKING:** The parking lot is on the south side of PA 741, just east of the Railroad Museum of Pennsylvania
- **HIGHLIGHTS:** Strasburg attractions, Amish farms

After you turn north on Fairview Road, you will be in Amish country. This ride is easy, and crossings of highways are protected by traffic lights. It is a loop northward out of Strasburg past the town of Bird in Hand, and through Intercourse and Paradise. You will see many large, prosperous Amish farms and some one-room schoolhouses.

As you ride through Amish country, you will occasionally see white barns with long, narrow sections of the siding hinged at the top and opened a couple of feet at the bottom. These are tobacco barns or drying sheds and have been part of the Lancaster County landscape for generations. Although tobacco acreage has decreased from 35,000 acres in the late 1950s to 9,000 acres today, about a thousand Amish and Mennonite families still raise $22 million of this crop each year, making it Lancaster County's largest cash crop. It's not for nothing that the Amish have referred to this crop as the "mortgage lifter." Until the late 1970s, Pennsylvania tobacco was the filler leaf of choice for premium cigars. Now other varieties are grown for cigarettes and chewing tobacco.

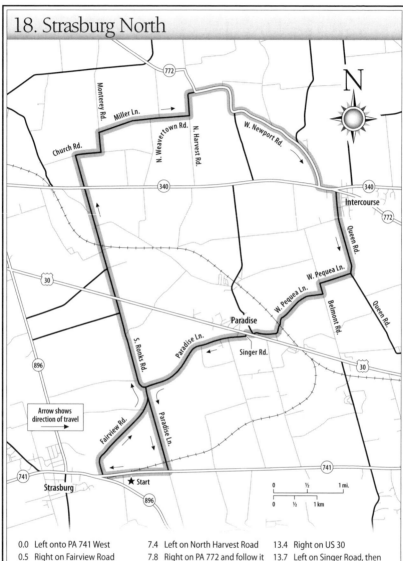

18. Strasburg North

0.0	Left onto PA 741 West	
0.5	Right on Fairview Road	
2.0	Left on South Ronks Road. Cross US 30, and then cross PA 340	
5.4	Right on Church Road	
5.7	Left on Monterey Road	
6.0	Right on Miller Lane	
6.4	Continue straight on North Weavertown Road	

7.4	Left on North Harvest Road
7.8	Right on PA 772 and follow it to Intercourse
10.3	At the intersection, turn left to remain on PA 772.
10.4	Right on Queen Road (no sign).
11.6	Right on West Pequea Lane
12.0	Left on Belmont Road
12.2	Right on West Pequea Lane

13.4	Right on US 30
13.7	Left on Singer Road, then immediately turn right on Paradise Lane
15.3	Bear left to stay on Paradise Lane.
16.6	Right on PA 741
17.0	Left into the parking lot

Paul Woodward, © The Countryman Press

Tobacco barn north of Strasburg

In the summer the crop is seen as a few neat acres of dark, lush leaves a few feet tall. Harvesting this crop is labor intensive, involving entire families in the effort. From late August through September, you may see Amish families together in the tobacco fields cutting the plants and then spearing them six at a time onto 4-foot-long wooden spears, then stacking them onto wagons drawn by teams of mules. The spears are then hung in the tobacco barns, where they are cured until late November. As you pass the barns, you may see the golden-brown plants hanging upside down from the spears.

Fewer families are continuing to grow tobacco because of the amount of labor involved and because of moral objections. The more conservative and traditional Amish are more likely to grow the leaf. Whatever you may think of tobacco, the sight of the harvest is picturesque.

0.0 Turn left out of the lot onto PA 741 West.

0.5 Turn right on Fairview Road.

2.0 Turn left on South Ronks Road. Cross US 30, and then cross PA 340.

About 0.1 mile before the turn onto South Ronks Road, Fairview Road becomes Paradise Lane, but there is no sign to indicate this. After you cross US 30, South Ronks Road becomes North Ronks Road.

5.4 Turn right on Church Road.

5.7 Turn left on Monterey Road.

6.0 Turn right on Miller Lane.

6.4 Continue straight on North Weavertown Road.

7.4 Turn left on North Harvest Road.

7.8 Turn right on PA 772 and follow it to the town of Intercourse.

10.3 At the intersection, turn left to remain on PA 772.
At this intersection, PA 340 and PA 772 merge for a short stretch. Be sure to take the right fork on PA 772.

10.4 Turn right on Queen Road.
A sign is notably absent at this turn.

11.6 Turn right on West Pequea Lane.

12.0 Turn left on Belmont Road.

12.2 Turn right on West Pequea Lane.

13.4 Turn right on US 30.

13.7 Turn left on Singer Road, then take an immediate right on Paradise Lane.

15.3 Bear left to stay on Paradise Lane.
South Ronks Road enters from the right.

16.6 Turn right on PA 741.

17.0 Turn left into the parking lot.

19

Strasburg South

- **DISTANCE:** 25 miles
- **TERRAIN/DIFFICULTY:** Rolling hills; easy to moderate
- **START:** Parking lot just east of the Railroad Museum of Pennsylvania on PA 741 in Strasburg
- **GPS COORDINATES OF START:** N39 58.947' / W76 09.525'
- **GETTING THERE/PARKING:** The parking lot is on the south side of PA 741 in Strasburg
- **HIGHLIGHTS:** Strasburg attractions, Amish farmland, expansive views of countryside

This ride shares the starting point with ride 18, and the two can easily be combined for a longer ride. It goes through the same kind of Amish farm country but is a little hillier, with some expansive and elevated views of the surrounding farmland from roads along the ridgelines.

After you turn left on PA 896, you will enjoy long views to the east and southwest until you turn right on Paradise Lane and descend into a little stream valley. Iva Road follows Little Beaver Creek for almost a mile, and after it turns into Mt. Pleasant Road you will climb out of the stream valley and regain the views of the countryside. For the rest of the loop back into Strasburg, the terrain is rolling hills with good views.

0.0 Turn left on PA 741 (Main Street).

0.6 Turn left on PA 896.

2.3 Turn right on Paradise Lane.

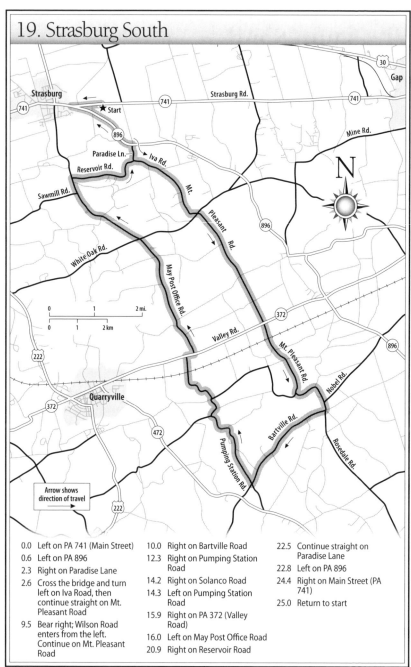

19. Strasburg South

Strasburg

Strasburg Rd.

741

741

30

Gap

896

Mine Rd.

★ Start

Paradise Ln.

Iva Rd.

Reservoir Rd.

Sawmill Rd.

Mt.

Pleasant Rd.

896

N

White Oak Rd.

May Post Office Rd.

372

896

0   1   2 mi.

0   1   2 km

Valley Rd.

Mt. Pleasant Rd.

222

Nobel Rd.

Quarryville

Pumping Station Rd.

Bartville Rd.

Rosedale Rd.

372

472

Arrow shows
direction of travel

222

0.0 Left on PA 741 (Main Street)	10.0 Right on Bartville Road	22.5 Continue straight on Paradise Lane
0.6 Left on PA 896	12.3 Right on Pumping Station Road	22.8 Left on PA 896
2.3 Right on Paradise Lane	14.2 Right on Solanco Road	24.4 Right on Main Street (PA 741)
2.6 Cross the bridge and turn left on Iva Road, then continue straight on Mt. Pleasant Road	14.3 Left on Pumping Station Road	25.0 Return to start
	15.9 Right on PA 372 (Valley Road)	
9.5 Bear right; Wilson Road enters from the left. Continue on Mt. Pleasant Road	16.0 Left on May Post Office Road	
	20.9 Right on Reservoir Road	

Paul Woodward, © The Countryman Press

Steam engines at the Railroad Museum of Pennsylvania, Strasburg

2.6 Cross the bridge and turn left on Iva Road, then continue straight on Mt. Pleasant Road.

Signage is confusing here; Iva and Mt. Pleasant roads continue together until Iva turns left at about 3.2 miles. Continue on Mt. Pleasant Road until the next turn at 9.5 miles.

9.5 Bear right; Wilson Road enters from the left. Continue on Mt. Pleasant Road.

10.0 Turn right on Bartville Road.

The signs say NOBLE ROAD at first, then transition to BARTVILLE ROAD.

12.3 Turn right on Pumping Station Road.

14.2 Turn right on Solanco Road.

14.3 Turn left on Pumping Station Road.

15.9 Turn right on PA 372 (Valley Road).

16.0 Turn left on May Post Office Road.

20.9 Turn right on Reservoir Road.

22.5 Continue straight on Paradise Lane.

22.8 Turn left on PA 896.

24.4 Turn right on Main Street (PA 741).

25.0 Return to start.

20. White Horse Road

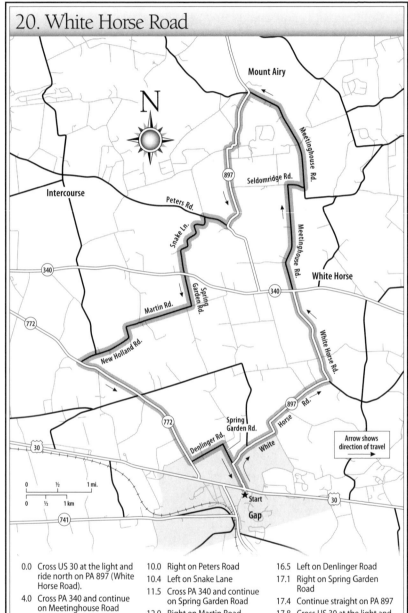

0.0 Cross US 30 at the light and ride north on PA 897 (White Horse Road).

4.0 Cross PA 340 and continue on Meetinghouse Road

5.6 Right on Seldomridge Road

5.9 Left on Meetinghouse Road

7.7 Left on PA 897

10.0 Right on Peters Road

10.4 Left on Snake Lane

11.5 Cross PA 340 and continue on Spring Garden Road

12.0 Right on Martin Road.

13.8 Left on New Holland Road

14.1 Left on PA 772

16.5 Left on Denlinger Road

17.1 Right on Spring Garden Road

17.4 Continue straight on PA 897

17.8 Cross US 30 at the light and return to the parking lot

20

White Horse Road

- **DISTANCE:** 17.8 miles
- **TERRAIN/DIFFICULTY:** Gentle, rolling hills; easy
- **START:** Mall parking lot at intersection of US 30 and PA 897
- **GPS COORDINATES OF START:** N39 59.451' / W76 01.032'
- **GETTING THERE/PARKING:** Immediately south of the traffic light at the intersection of US 30 and PA 897 is a shopping mall with a large parking lot.
- **HIGHLIGHTS:** Amish farming country, Amish schoolhouses, horse-drawn carriages

The area traversed by this ride is pure Amish farm country. You will notice that the asphalt pavement on these roads is polished by the narrow iron tires of buggies. As soon as you leave US 30 and start north on PA 897, except for a few cars on the road, you will see virtually nothing but human- and animal-powered machinery. There are even roads that do not have utility poles.

On many of these country roads you will encounter Amish buggies, of which there are a number of styles reflecting regional and religious differences. For example, some orders forbid whipsockets and dashboards as frivolous adornments, while others tolerate cartoon figures stuck to the insides of the windows. Something to contemplate is where these carriages come from. You won't see big buggy dealerships along the roads, and carriage manufacture is so specialized—with many handcrafted components—that each farmer would be unable to make his own.

About half of the Amish in this area are farmers, and another small percentage engage in some additional enterprise to supplement farming. Farming carries the highest prestige of any occupation among the Amish, with craft industries a distant second. A little more than a third of the Amish here have small industry as their primary occupation. They try to keep their businesses small, and once a business employs more than 28 people, the owner is encouraged to sell it to an outside concern, as it is then considered to be a religious liability. If you know where to look, you can find carriage, carpentry, furniture building, harness, and blacksmith shops, which sometimes employ entire families. The Amish have a deserved reputation for conscientious craftsmanship.

After winding north on PA 897, you will cross PA 340 at 4.0 miles and continue straight ahead on Meetinghouse Road, which gradually returns you to PA 897. After riding south on PA 897 for a little over 2 miles, you will turn right on Peters Road, then left on felicitously named Snake Lane, which has six sharp, fun curves in the space of about a mile. Crossing PA 340 again, you proceed south on Spring Garden Road and then left on Martin Road. The remainder of the ride is a loop back to the start. This includes about 2.5 miles on PA 772 and a short stretch of country road back to PA 897.

0.0 Cross US 30 at the light and ride north on PA 897 (White Horse Road).

4.0 Cross PA 340 and continue on Meetinghouse Road.

5.6 Turn right on Seldomridge Road.

5.9 Turn left on Meetinghouse Road.

7.7 Turn left on PA 897.

10.0 Turn right on Peters Road.

10.4 Turn left on Snake Lane.
This road is curvy and fun to ride.

11.5 Cross PA 340 and continue on Spring Garden Road.

12.0 Turn right on Martin Road.
Signage is confusing here. Martin Road becomes Hershey Church Road, and then South New Holland Road.

Amish schoolhouse

13.8 Turn left on New Holland Road.

The sign here clearly names this segment of road as New Holland Road.

14.1 Turn left on PA 772.

16.5 Turn left on Denlinger Road.

17.1 Turn right on Spring Garden Road.

17.4 Continue straight on PA 897.

17.8 Cross US 30 at the light and return to the parking lot.

21. Katze Boucle Weeg

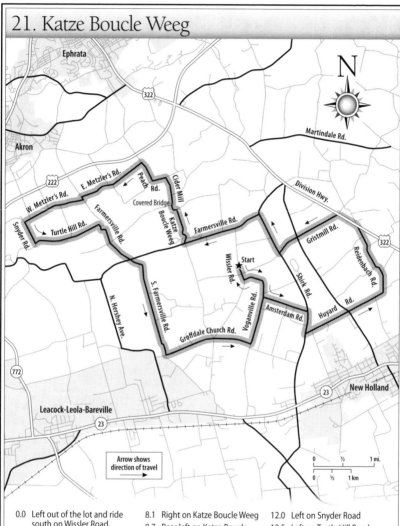

Arrow shows direction of travel

0   ½   1 mi.
0   ½   1 km

0.0 Left out of the lot and ride south on Wissler Road	8.1 Right on Katze Boucle Weeg	12.0 Left on Snyder Road
0.2 Left on Voganville Road	8.7 Bear left on Katze Boucle Weeg	12.5 Left on Turtle Hill Road
0.7 Left on Amsterdam Road	8.9 Cross the covered bridge and continue straight on Cider Mill Road	6.6 Right on Farmersville Road, cross Conestoga Creek, and continue straight on South Farmersville Road
1.5 Right on Shirk Road		
1.8 Left on Huyard Road		
3.2 Left on Reidenbach Road	9.3 Left on Peach Road.	
4.5 Left on US 322	9.4 Right to continue on Peach Road	16.1 Left on Groffdale Church Road
4.9 Left on Gristmill Road		
6.2 Right on North Shirk Road	8.8 Left on East Metzler's Road	6.6 Left on Voganville Road
6.8 Left on Farmersville Road	11.0 Left on Farmersville Road, then immediately turn right onto West Metzler's Road	19.0 Right on Wissler Road
		2.2 Turn into parking lot

21

Katze Boucle Weeg

DISTANCE: 19.2 miles

TERRAIN/DIFFICULTY: Rolling hills, one short, sharp hill; easy to moderate

START: Parking lot of Village Chapel on Wissler Road

GPS COORDINATES OF START: N40 07.583' / W76 07.846'

GETTING THERE/PARKING: The Village Chapel is on the right side of Wissler Road, less than 0.1 mile north of its intersection with Linden Grove Road. Please do not park here during Sunday services. The center of the city of Ephrata is the intersection of US 322 and PA 272. Drive about 5.5 miles southeast on US 322 and turn right on Gristmill Road, which becomes Linden Grove Road in 1 mile after it crosses North Shirk Road. Wissler Road is the next crossroad and is about 0.75 mile past Shirk Road. Turn right on Wissler Road and look for the chapel on the right. If you are driving from US 30, depending upon how far east or west you are, you can take US 222, US 322, PA 897, or PA 10 toward Ephrata and find Gristmill Road on US 322. This is in the middle of nowhere, but it's really not that hard to find when you consult a map.

HIGHLIGHTS: Amish farms, covered bridge

The goal of this ride is to spend a couple of hours in the fine Amish countryside and to enjoy this splendid little road in northern Lancaster County. I am fascinated by road names and discovered this one while examining a map with a magnifying glass. I *had* to find it. When I'm riding, I tend to avoid roads like Agony Hill Road and find myself attracted to River Road or Creek Road as the names generally tell

something about the terrain. There are also road names that in themselves arouse curiosity: how did Ground Hog College Road get its name, or why is a road in the middle of the countryside called 18th Street?

Katze Boucle Weeg means "Cat's Back Road" in Pennsylvania German, also called Pennsilfannisch Deitsch, Pennsylvania Dutch, or Pennsylvania German, a dialect of High German. (I have seen several variants of the spelling of this road name and have decided to accept the one on the road sign.) The ancestral home of most of the Amish is the Rhineland-Palatinate region of Germany; Pennsylvania German is related to the dialect once spoken there and contains elements of southwest German and Swiss dialects as well. Old Order Amish and Old Order Mennonites still use it in their everyday speech.

Katze Boucle Weeg is less than a mile long and crosses a sharp little ridge that gives it the profile of an angry cat. It's fun to ride, and at the bottom on the north side is a covered bridge. Except for a short segment on US 322, you will see nothing but countryside on this ride. After you climb the south side of Katze Boucle Weeg and descend the hill, you will cross the Bitzer's Mill Covered Bridge, which spans Conestoga Creek. Watch your map carefully for the next couple of miles; road signs are either absent or confusing when not absent. You will keep pretty close company with Conestoga Creek for 5 miles and, after crossing a bridge, will return to the open countryside to complete the loop back to the start.

0.0 Turn left out of the parking lot and ride south on Wissler Road.

0.2 Turn left on Voganville Road.

0.7 Turn left on Amsterdam Road.

1.5 Turn right on Shirk Road.

1.8 Turn left on Huyard Road.

3.2 Turn left on Reidenbach Road.

4.5 Turn left on US 322.

4.9 Turn left on Gristmill Road.

6.2 Turn right on North Shirk Road.

6.8 Turn left on Farmersville Road.

8.1 Turn right on Katze Boucle Weeg.

8.7 Bear left on Katze Boucle Weeg.

8.9 Cross the covered bridge and continue straight on Cider Mill Road.

9.3 Turn left on Peach Road.
This is a T intersection.

9.4 Turn right to continue on Peach Road.

9.8 Turn left on East Metzler's Road.

11.0 Turn left on Farmersville Road, then take an immediate right onto West Metzler's Road.

12.0 Turn left on Snyder Road.

12.5 Turn left on Turtle Hill Road.

13.6 Turn right on Farmersville Road, cross Conestoga Creek, and continue straight on South Farmersville Road.

16.1 Turn left on Groffdale Church Road.

17.6 Turn left on Voganville Road.

19.0 Turn right on Wissler Road.

19.2 Turn into the parking lot.

22

Robert Fulton House

- **DISTANCE:** 21.4 miles
- **TERRAIN/DIFFICULTY:** Rolling hills; easy
- **START:** Parking lot behind the Robert Fulton House, on the west side of US 222 and south of Quarryville
- **GPS COORDINATES OF START:** N39 48.337' / W76 09.592'
- **GETTING THERE/PARKING:** From the intersection of PA 372 and US 222 in Quarryville, take US 222 south and look for the Robert Fulton House on the right in about 6.5 miles. The parking lot is behind the house.
- **HIGHLIGHTS:** Fulton birthplace, Amish farms, ride along West Branch of Octoraro Creek

This ride begins in the rear parking lot of the Fulton Birthplace, operated by the Southern Lancaster County Historical Society, which offers tours on Saturday and Sunday between Memorial Day and Labor Day. The site's gardens are simple, attractive, and well maintained. Robert Fulton is remembered as the inventor of the steamship; however, rather than inventing the steamship, he developed a commercially successful example that he demonstrated in Paris in 1803. Napoleon was so impressed with it that he commissioned Fulton to design a submarine for him. Returning to the United States, Fulton built the *Clermont,* which successfully navigated the Hudson River to Albany. In addition to his engineering triumphs, he was a trained artist and painted portraits of notable Americans of his day.

The countryside around the Fulton House is mostly Amish farm-land, and you will probably see many Amish children returning home

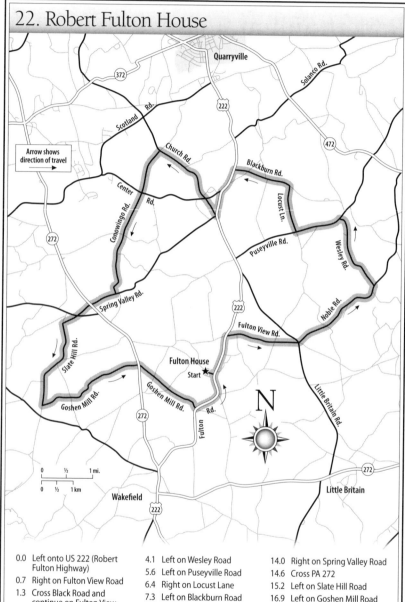

22. Robert Fulton House

Quarryville

Arrow shows direction of travel

Scotland Rd.

Church Rd.

Blackburn Rd.

Locust Ln.

Center Rd.

Conowingo Rd.

Puseyville Rd.

Wesley Rd.

Spring Valley Rd.

Noble Rd.

Fulton View Rd.

Slate Hill Rd.

Fulton House
Start

Goshen Mill Rd.

Goshen Mill Rd.

Fulton Rd.

Little Britain Rd.

N

Wakefield

Little Britain

0   ½   1 mi.
0   ½   1 km

0.0 Left onto US 222 (Robert Fulton Highway)	4.1 Left on Wesley Road	14.0 Right on Spring Valley Road
0.7 Right on Fulton View Road	5.6 Left on Puseyville Road	14.6 Cross PA 272
1.3 Cross Black Road and continue on Fulton View Road	6.4 Right on Locust Lane	15.2 Left on Slate Hill Road
	7.3 Left on Blackburn Road	16.9 Left on Goshen Mill Road
2.1 Cross Little Britain Road and continue on Noble Road	8.4 Left on US 222	20.5 Left on Fulton Road (Robert Fulton Highway / US 222)
	9.4 Right and back on Church Road	
	11.1 Left on Conowingo Road	21.4 Left into parking lot

Paul Woodward. © The Countryman Press

Robert Fulton House

from school if you ride on a weekday afternoon. You turn left out the parking lot and ride north on PA 222, which has smooth pavement and not much traffic. Turn right on Fulton View Road and begin a large counterclockwise loop through the countryside and back to the start. At 4.1 miles you pass the tiny town of Kings Bridge and begin a very pleasant ride in the Octoraro Creek Valley.

0.0 Turn left out of the parking lot onto US 222 (Robert Fulton Highway).

0.7 Turn right on Fulton View Road.

1.3 Cross Black Road and continue on Fulton View Road.
Signage is confusing here.

2.1 Cross Little Britain Road and continue on Noble Road.

4.1 Turn left on Wesley Road.

5.6 Turn left on Puseyville Road.

6.4 Turn right on Locust Lane.

7.3 Turn left on Blackburn Road.

8.4 Turn left on US 222.

9.4 Turn right and back on Church Road.

11.1 Turn left on Conowingo Road.

14.0 Turn right on Spring Valley Road.

14.6 Cross PA 272.

15.2 Turn left on Slate Hill Road.

16.9 Turn left on Goshen Mill Road.

20.5 Turn left on Fulton Road (Robert Fulton Highway/US 222).

21.4 Turn left into the Robert Fulton House parking lot.

SUSQUEHANNA VALLEY

*Spectacular view of the southern Susquehanna River
from Mount Pisgah*

THE LAST THREE RIDES IN THIS BOOK are in the Susquehanna River Valley, although ride 25 starts in Strasburg before descending into the valley. They will give you a fair sample of this great river valley, which forms the border between Lancaster and York counties. At this point in its course the river is about a mile wide and flows southeast into Maryland, where it empties into the Chesapeake Bay at Havre de Grace, providing about half of the bay's freshwater inflow.

It is an ancient river, older than the mountains through which it flows. At 444 miles long, it is the longest river on the American East Coast. The North Branch begins in an unprepossessing stream at the south end of Otsego (Glimmerglass) Lake in Cooperstown, New York, and flows southwest through Pennsylvania's anthracite region until it is joined by the smaller West Branch near Sunbury.

There are three hydroelectric dams on the river south of Lancaster, and ride 24 allows you to see the oldest of them from a dramatic over-look. Although the river once supported a lot of industry and barge transportation, this section is now heavily wooded right up to the high bluffs above it. The bluffs on the east bank provide significant chal-lenges to bicyclists, and I have chosen to avoid most of these. (I once rode from Harrisburg to Sunbury along the east bank, and it was one of the most strenuous rides I've ever taken, a relentless succession of climbs and descents over the entire 60-plus miles. On another outing I made a lung-busting ascent to the village of Highville, located south of ride 23, and I can only imagine that the person who named it arrived on a bicycle.) The only long climb in these three rides is in ride 23, the one to Sam Lewis State Park on the west bank, and it really isn't too bad. At the park you will be rewarded with a commanding view of the beautiful river valley to the south and the bridges to the north.

Tourism Information

www.columbiapa.org

www.rivertowns.com

www.bbonline.com

www.aboutlancaster.com

www.shwpc.com (Safe Harbor Water Power Corporation Web site)

www.localhikes.com (Tucquan Glenn hikes)

www.lancasterconservancy.org

www.muddyrunpark.com

Bicycle Shops

Bike Line of Lancaster, 117 Rohrerstown Road, Lancaster; 717-394-8998

The Cycle Works, 206 Hellam Street, Wrightsville; 717-252-1509

23

Sam Lewis State Park

- **DISTANCE**: 23.2 miles

- **TERRAIN/DIFFICULTY**: Level along the river, with a strenuous climb to the park; moderate

- **START**: Central Manor Elementary School, on PA 999 about 3.5 miles west of Millersville

- **GPS COORDINATES OF START**: N40 00.006' / W76 25.485'

- **GETTING THERE/PARKING**: PA 999 runs from Lancaster, through Millersville, and ends at PA 441 at the riverbank. Take PA 999 about 3.5 miles west out of Millersville; the school is on your left.

- **HIGHLIGHTS**: Spectacular views of the southern Susquehanna River from the summit of Mount Pisgah in the state park

At 885 feet above sea level, the summit of Mount Pisgah in Samuel S. Lewis State Park is the highest point in the vicinity and offers spectacular, unobstructed views of the southern Susquehanna River. The river is about a mile wide at this point in its course from New York State to the Chesapeake Bay. The current bridge that spans this section of the river is listed as a Historic Civil Engineering Landmark and is considered the world's longest concrete multiple-arch bridge. Including the spans over land, this bridge is 7,344 feet long; it is properly named the Veterans Memorial Bridge, although locals call it the Columbia-Wrightsville Bridge.

The original bridge on this site was completed in 1814, and at the time it was the longest covered bridge in the world, at 5,690 feet. It was destroyed by ice and flooding in 1832. The wooden structure that replaced it in 1834 was burned by Union militia during the Civil War

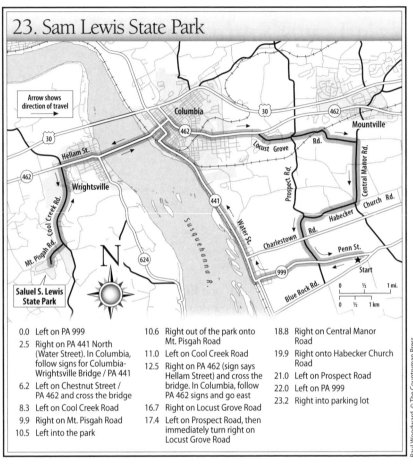

23. Sam Lewis State Park

Arrow shows direction of travel

Columbia

Mountville

Hellam St.

Wrightsville

Cool Creek Rd.

Mt. Pisgah Rd.

Locust Grove Rd.

Prospect Rd.

Central Manor Rd.

Church Rd.

Habecker

Water St.

Charlestown Rd.

Penn St.

Saluel S. Lewis State Park

Susquehanna R.

Blue Rock Rd.

Start

N

0   ½   1 mi.
0   ½   1 km

0.0   Left on PA 999

2.5   Right on PA 441 North (Water Street). In Columbia, follow signs for Columbia-Wrightsville Bridge / PA 441

6.2   Left on Chestnut Street / PA 462 and cross the bridge

8.3   Left on Cool Creek Road

9.9   Right on Mt. Pisgah Road

10.5 Left into the park

10.6 Right out of the park onto Mt. Pisgah Road

11.0 Left on Cool Creek Road

12.5 Right on PA 462 (sign says Hellam Street) and cross the bridge. In Columbia, follow PA 462 signs and go east

16.7 Right on Locust Grove Road

17.4 Left on Prospect Road, then immediately turn right on Locust Grove Road

18.8 Right on Central Manor Road

19.9 Right onto Habecker Church Road

21.0 Left on Prospect Road

22.0 Left on PA 999

23.2 Right into parking lot

Paul Woodward, © The Countryman Press

to keep Confederate troops from crossing the river.

The state park is in York County, but the ride begins across the river in Lancaster County. You ride 2.5 miles mostly downhill to the river and turn right on PA 441 (also called Water Street), which is flat along the river. In the town of Columbia, follow the COLUMBIA-WRIGHTSVILLE BRIDGE/PA 441 signs. The bridge begins as Chestnut Street in town and crosses the river as PA 462. After crossing the river and turning left on Cool Creek Road, you soon start the 1-mile climb up to the park. In addition to providing great views, the fields in the park are good for picnics and kite flying. Leaving the park, you retrace your route back across the river and continue through the west part of

Columbia until you turn right on Locust Grove Road. The next 6.4 miles traverse high, open countryside above the east bank of the river and take you back to the school.

0.0 Turn left on PA 999.

2.5 Turn right on PA 441 North (Water Street). In the town of Columbia, follow the the COLUMBIA-WRIGHTSVILLE BRIDGE/PA 441 signs.
PA 441 follows the course of the river.

6.2 Turn left on Chestnut Street/PA 462 and cross the bridge.

8.3 Turn left on Cool Creek Road.
The climb begins on Cool Creek Road at 9.2 miles.

9.9 Turn right on Mt. Pisgah Road.
The climb continues on Mt. Pisgah Road and into the park.

10.5 Turn left into the park.
There is currently no entrance fee for the park. The best view is from the grassy crown of Mount Pisgah east of the picnic pavilion.

10.6 Turn right out of the park onto Mt. Pisgah Road.

View of the lower Susquehanna River bridges from Mount Pisgah

11.0 Turn left on Cool Creek Road.

12.5 Turn right on PA 462 (the sign says HELLAM STREET) and follow it back across the bridge. In Columbia, follow the signs for PA 462 and follow it east.

16.7 Turn right on Locust Grove Road.

17.4 Turn left on Prospect Road, then take an immediate right to continue on Locust Grove Road.

18.8 Turn right on Central Manor Road.

19.9 Turn right onto Habecker Church Road.

21.0 Turn left on Prospect Road.

22.0 Turn left on PA 999.

23.2 Turn right into the school parking lot.

24

Muddy Run—Holtwood Dam

- **DISTANCE:** 13.1 miles
- **TERRAIN/DIFFICULTY:** Hilly; moderate
- **START:** State game land parking area on the right side of County Route 3006, 0.4 mile from the entrance to Muddy Run Recreation Park
- **GPS COORDINATES OF START:** N39 49.416' / W76 18.461'
- **GETTING THERE/PARKING:** Take PA 372 west out of Quarryville; cross PA 272 in the town of Buck. About 5 miles past this intersection, enter Muddy Run Recreation Park at the Exelon sign on the left. The parking lot is 0.4 mile along this road, on the right just before the dam.
- **HIGHLIGHTS:** Holtwood hydroelectric dam, Muddy Run Recreation Park, view of river from observation area, frequent sightings of bald eagles

This short, hilly ride begins in the 700-acre Muddy Run Recreation Park, which provides year-round camping facilities. The 100-acre Muddy Run Reservoir is open to fishing and human-powered watercraft. Ride straight across the dam, which is part of a pumped storage power-generating facility; the reservoir is on your left and the river on your right. Pass the signs for the campground entrance and turn onto Furniss Road. Turn left on Susquehannock Drive, and continue for about 3 miles on this pleasant little road. You will turn left on PA 372, and in about 1.9 miles turn onto Old Holtwood Road on your right. In another 1.9 miles you will take a left turn and climb a steep 0.4-mile hill to the Holtwood Face Rock Observation Area, which gives the best view of the dam.

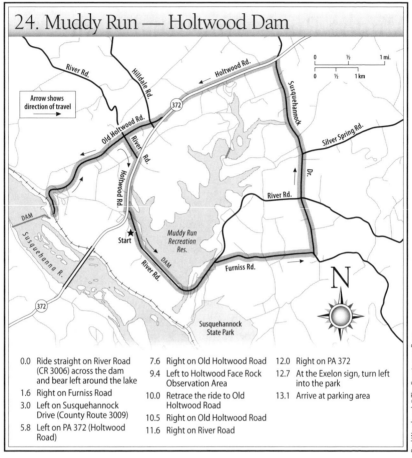

24. Muddy Run — Holtwood Dam

Arrow shows direction of travel

0.0	Ride straight on River Road (CR 3006) across the dam and bear left around the lake	
1.6	Right on Furniss Road	
3.0	Left on Susquehannock Drive (County Route 3009)	
5.8	Left on PA 372 (Holtwood Road)	
7.6	Right on Old Holtwood Road	
9.4	Left to Holtwood Face Rock Observation Area	
10.0	Retrace the ride to Old Holtwood Road	
10.5	Right on Old Holtwood Road	
11.6	Right on River Road	
12.0	Right on PA 372	
12.7	At the Exelon sign, turn left into the park	
13.1	Arrive at parking area	

Paul Woodward, © The Countryman Press

Holtwood Dam is the oldest of the three major hydroelectric dams built across the lower Susquehanna River. It was constructed between 1905 and 1910, and impounds Lake Aldred to the north. At its western end is a fish lift that allows shad and other migratory fish to travel upriver to their spawning grounds. White-water kayakers enjoy the rapids immediately below the dam, and bald eagles are frequently seen soaring above this part of the river.

Allow some time after your ride to drive north on River Road to see Tucquan Glenn Nature Preserve and take in the views from Pinnacle Rock, just a few miles north.

0.0 Ride straight on River Road (CR 3006) across the dam and bear left around the foot of the lake.

1.6 Turn right on Furniss Road.

3.0 Turn left on Susquehannock Drive (County Route 3009).

5.8 Turn left on PA 372 (Holtwood Road).

7.6 Turn right on Old Holtwood Road.

9.4 Turn left to Holtwood Face Rock Observation Area.
This is a steep little climb on a paved road. The observation area has the best available view of the dam. Roads closer to the river have been closed for security reasons, even though they appear on many maps.

10.0 Retrace the ride out of the parking area to Old Holtwood Road.

10.5 Turn right on Old Holtwood Road.

11.6 Turn right on River Road.

12.0 Turn right on PA 372.

12.7 At the Exelon sign, turn left into the park.

13.1 Arrive back at the parking area.

Holtwood hydroelectric dam from Holtwood Face Rock Observation Area

25. Safe Harbor

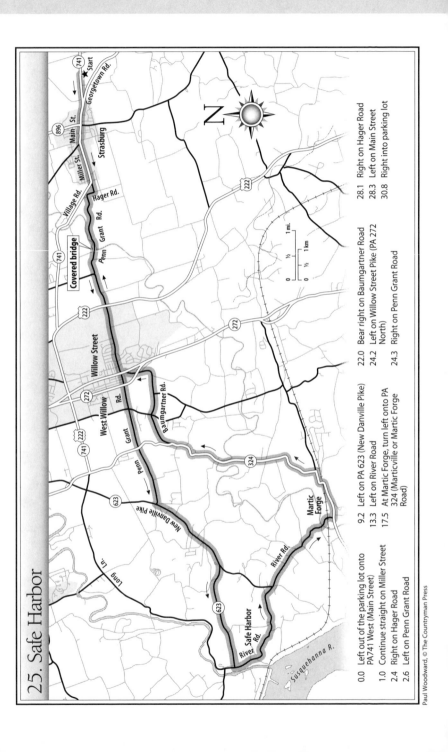

0.0	Left out of the parking lot onto PA741 West (Main Street)
1.0	Continue straight on Miller Street
2.4	Right on Hager Road
2.6	Left on Penn Grant Road
9.2	Left on PA 623 (New Danville Pike)
13.3	Left on River Road
17.5	At Martic Forge, turn left onto PA 324 (Marticville or Martic Forge Road)
22.0	Bear right on Baumgartner Road
24.2	Left on Willow Street Pike (PA 272 North)
24.3	Right on Penn Grant Road
28.1	Right on Hager Road
28.3	Left on Main Street
30.8	Right into parking lot

Paul Woodward, © The Countryman Press

25

Safe Harbor

- **DISTANCE:** 30.8 miles
- **TERRAIN/DIFFICULTY:** Rolling hills; easy to moderate
- **START:** Parking lot of the Railroad Museum of Pennsylvania, Strasburg
- **GPS COORDINATES OF START:** N39 58.947' / W76 09.525'
- **GETTING THERE/PARKING:** The parking lot is on the south side of PA 741, immediately east of the Railroad Museum of Pennsylvania
- **HIGHLIGHTS:** Descents and climbs in the Susquehanna River Valley, town of Safe Harbor, Neff's Mill Covered Bridge, Strasburg attractions

This ride starts at the same point as rides 18 and 19, but the destination is in the river valley. Ride west on PA 741, which becomes Main Street and then Miller Street in the old town of Strasburg. Leaving the west side of this picturesque town, you ride west on Penn Grant Road, which is a pleasant 6.6-mile stretch of open country road. You will cross the Neff's Mill Covered Bridge at 3.7 miles.

When you turn left on Main Street (PA 623) at mile 9.2, you start the 4.1-mile descent into the Susquehanna Valley, ending up in the town of Safe Harbor. The transition from the sunny, open uplands to the deep shade of the river valley is dramatic, especially on a warm summer day.

This picturesque little town near the confluence of Conestoga Creek and the Susquehanna River is a small remnant of its former self. In the 1850s it was a bustling industrial center containing a blast furnace, iron foundry, and rolling mill. The wrought-iron cannon, a major

Neff's Mill Covered Bridge

advance in weapons technology, was invented here in 1855. There are few traces of this time, and Safe Harbor is now a quiet, leafy little community.

Nearby Safe Harbor Dam is the northernmost of the three lower Susquehanna dams impounding Lake Clarke to the north. Like its much larger neighbor, Holtwood Dam, it was built with fish ladders to accommodate migratory fish. The community experienced a brief resurgence during its construction in 1930–1931.

After passing through Safe Harbor, you will gradually circle back to Penn Grant Road from the south and return through Strasburg to the start. The climb out of the river valley is gradual.

0.0 Turn left out of the parking lot onto PA 741 West (Main Street).

1.0 Continue straight on Miller Street.
In the center of Strasburg, Main Street changes its name to Miller Street.

2.4 Turn right on Hager Road.

2.6 Turn left on Penn Grant Road.

Neff's Mill Covered Bridge is at 3.7 miles.

9.2 Turn left on PA 623 (New Danville Pike).
This road is called Main Street as it approaches the Susquehanna River.

13.3 Turn left on River Road.
There is a shady park, and just beyond it on the left is Safe Harbor Village.

17.5 At Martic Forge, turn left onto PA 324 (Marticville or Martic Forge Road).

22.0 Bear right on Baumgartner Road.

24.2 Turn left on Willow Street Pike (PA 272 North).

24.3 Turn right on Penn Grant Road.

28.1 Turn right on Hager Road

28.3 Turn left on Main Street.

30.8 Turn right into parking lot.